Embroidery
from the
Heart

Embroidery
from the
Heart

Heart Foundation

SALLYMILNER
PUBLISHING

First published in 2002 by
Sally Milner Publishing Pty Ltd
PO Box 2104
Bowral NSW 2576
AUSTRALIA

© National Heart Foundation of Australia (NSW DIVISION) 2002

Design: Anna Warren, Warren Ventures Pty Ltd
Editing: Anne Savage
Photography: Tim Connolly

Printed in China

National Library of Australia Cataloguing-in-Publication data:
Embroidery from the heart.

 ISBN 1 86351 307 8.

 1. Embroidery - Patterns. 2. Heart in art. I. National
Heart Foundation of Australia. (Series : Milner craft series).

 746.44041

10 9 8 7 6 5 4 3 2 1

Contents

Introduction

*T*he tragic and untimely death of a young woman has inspired a touching memorial to her, and a creative exploration of the importance of the heart in all our lives.

A wonderful book of treasures for your enjoyment, *Embroidery from the Heart* is a stunning collection of pieces created around the theme of the heart.

Kerry Teulan died suddenly of a heart attack at the age of 37, leaving her husband and two young children. Her close friend Bernadette Janson wanted to commemorate Kerry's life and focus attention on the dangers of heart disease. An embroiderer for twenty years, Bernadette decided her project should focus on embroidery. She asked some of Australia's best-known embroiderers to design heart themed creations and donate them to the Heart Foundation. Kerry's family embraced the idea as a loving tribute to her.

The seeds of *Embroidery from the Heart* were sown in sadness but Bernadette's idea grew with love and quickly found a strength of its own. She approached the Heart Foundation in Sydney, which was delighted to be part of the project. Despite a steady decline in death rates from heart disease and stroke over the past twenty years, heart disease still claims more than 50 000 lives a year.

Bernadette received an overwhelming reply from embroiderers eager to participate. 'I was amazed at the positive response,' she said.

Many of the embroiderers were particularly keen to contribute having experienced first-hand the loss of a family member or close friend from heart disease. The contributors come from all over Australia, indicating the degree to which the ravages of heart disease touch us all.

For Bernadette, the project provided a practical outlet for grieving as well as a way of helping the Heart Foundation in its efforts to prevent heart disease and stroke. 'Hearts feature a lot in embroidery designs and I thought it would be good to make people think about what a heart is.' Bernadette feels that the pieces and their tragic genesis poignantly remind us how important it is to have a healthy heart.

She composed a poem titled 'Matters of the Heart' to provide inspiration for the embroiderers.

It is a beautiful thread that binds us
With that thread
May you stitch with love
And generosity
And know
That it is giving such as yours
That makes our hearts light
And our spirits sing

Embroidery from the Heart has toured Art and Craft fairs throughout Australia raising funds for the Heart Foundation and increasing awareness about heart disease. The embroidery pieces have been either auctioned or raffled to raise funds for the Foundation, and a proportion of the proceeds from this book will also go to the Foundation to support education and research into the prevention and treatment of heart disease.

There is no need to detail further Bernadette's tremendous commitment to Kerry, nor her devotion to the cause of furthering knowledge about heart disease. For these pieces, conceived in love and dedicated to life, say everything.

Embroidery from the Heart is a tribute in embroidery—to one heart from many.

Annie's rose
(*And Time Remembered is Grief Forgotten*)

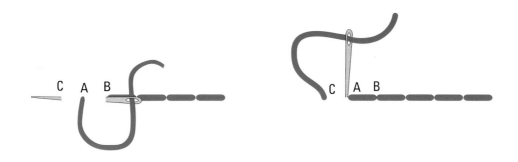

Back stitch
(*Evening Bag, A Garden in My Heart, And Time Remembered is Grief Forgotten, Heart Flutter, Treasured Heart, Redwork! AWork of Heart, My Heart Blooms in My Garden, Friendship Heart*)

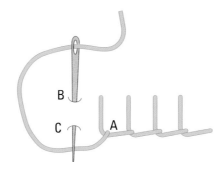

Blanket stitch
(*Evening Bag, Hearts and Butterfly, Heart Flutter*)

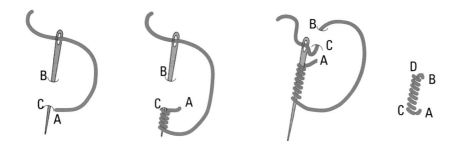

Bullion knot (Bullion stitch)
(*Evening Bag, Hearts and Butterfly, A Garden in My Heart, Heart Flutter, Treasured Heart, My Heart Blooms in My Garden, Friendship Heart*)

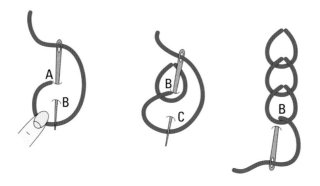

Chain stitch
(*My Heart Blooms in My Garden, Friendship Heart*)

Colonial knot
(*And Time Remembered is Grief Forgotten*)

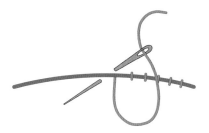

Couching
(*Hearts and Butterfly*)

Detached chain stitch
(*Evening Bag, A Garden in My Heart, Friendship Heart*)

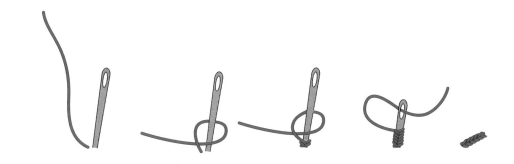

Drizzle stitch
(*Heart Flutter*)

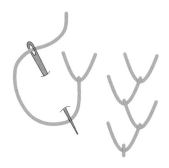

Feather stitch
(*Treasured Heart, Lace and Latticework, My Heart Blooms in My Garden*)

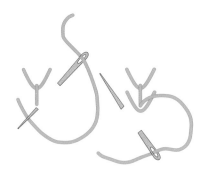

Fly stitch
(*Evening Bag, A Garden in My Heart, And Time Remembered is Grief Forgotten,
My Heart Blooms in My Garden, Friendship Heart*)

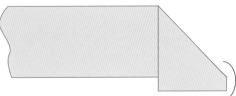

1. Fold ribbon over approximately at a
right angle, leaving a small tail

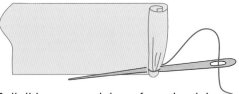

2. Roll ribbon several times from the right
until the fold is covered, stitching
through each layer to secure

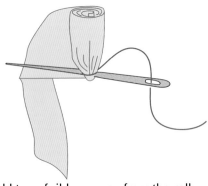

3. Fold top of ribbon away from the roll;
keep rolling until fold is covered,
continuing to securely stitch each layer;
repeat until rose is required size

4. For a small rosebud, make only
two or three rolls

Folded ribon rose
(*Treasured Heart*)

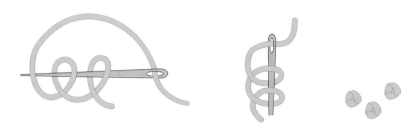

French knot
(*Evening Bag, A Garden in My Heart, And Time Remembered is Grief Forgotten, Heart Flutter, Lace and Latticework, Redwork! A Work of Heart, My Heart Blooms in My Garden, Friendship Heart, Valentine Roses*)

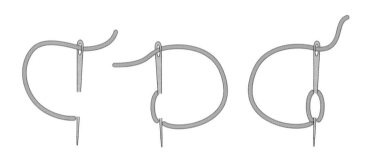

Granitos
(*Friendship Heart*)

Herringbone stitch
(*My Heart Blooms in My Garden*)

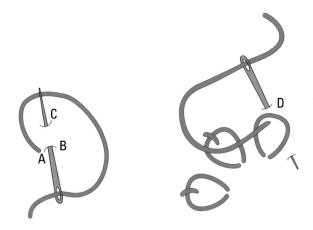

Lazy daisy stitch
(*Heart Christening Robe, A Garden in My Heart, Heart Flutter, Valentine Roses*)

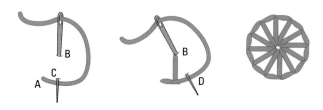

Lazy daisy buttonhole
(*My Heart Blooms in My Garden*)

Long and short stitch
(*Evening Bag, Heart Flutter*)

Loop stitch
(*Valentine Roses*)

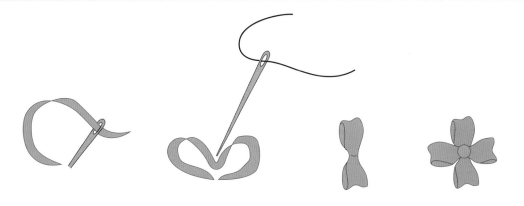

Loop stitch flowers
(*My Heart Blooms in My Garden*)

Pekinese stitch
(*Redwork! A Work of Heart*)

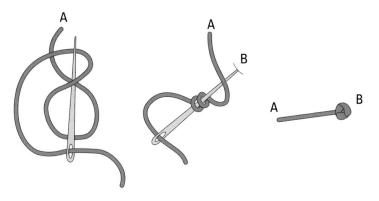

Pistil stitch
(*Heart Flutter*)

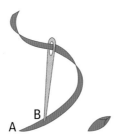

Ribbon stitch
(*Heart of Roses, Heart Flutter, Lace and Latticework, My Heart Blooms in My Garden, Valentine Roses*)

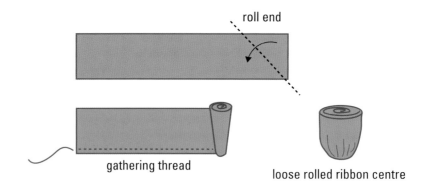

Rolled ribbon roses
(*Valentine Roses*)

Running stitch
(*Hearts and Butterfly, A Garden in My Heart*)

Satin stitch
(*Evening Bag, Hearts and Butterfly, Heart Flutter*)

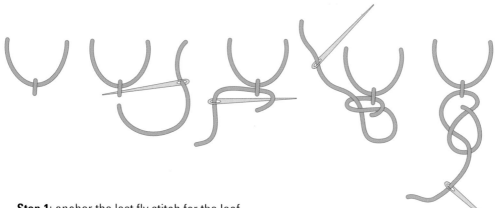

Step 1: anchor the last fly stitch for the leaf
Step 2: re-emerge below the last fly stitch, very close to it, then pass the needle from
right to left under the last anchor stitch, without piercing the fabric, and leave a small loop
Step 3: pass the needle back through this loop from left to right, thus creating a second loop
Step 4: take the needle in a clockwise motion up through the second loop
Step 5: to tighten the knot, turn your wrist to the right as you pull, thus creating a figure of eight

Smocker's knot
(*And Time Remembered is Grief Forgotten*)

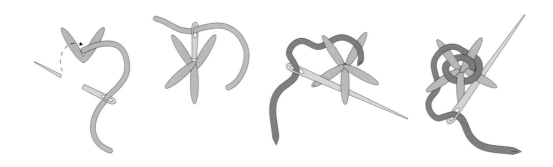

Spider's web rose (woven rose, wound ribbon rose)
(*Heart Christening Robe, And Time Remembered is Grief Forgotten, Lace and Latticework*)

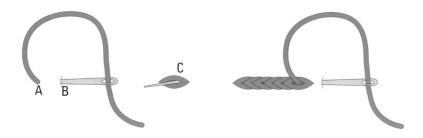

Split stitch
(*Hearts and Butterfly*)

Stem stitch
(*Evening Bag, And Time Remembered is Grief Forgotten, Heart Flutter, Lace and Latticework, My Heart Blooms in My Garden*)

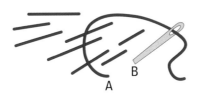

Straight stitch
(*Evening Bag, A Garden in My Heart, And Time Remembered is Grief Forgotten, Heart Flutter, Lace and Latticework, My Heart Blooms in My Garden, Friendship Heart, Valentine Heart*)

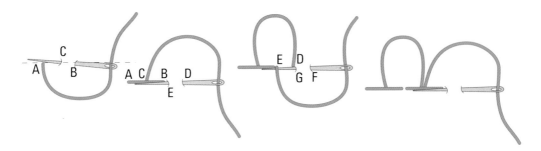

Turkey stitch
(*Heart Flutter*)

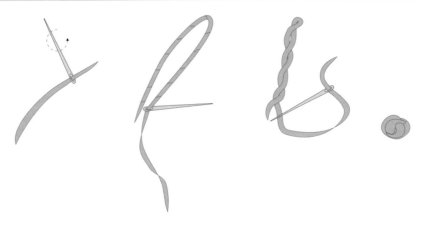

Twirled rose
(*And Time Remembered is Grief Forgotten, My Heart Blooms in My Garden*)

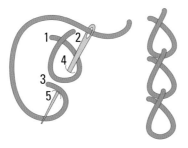

Twisted chain stitch
(*Evening Bag*)

Twisted straight stitch
(*Valentine Roses*)

Whip stitch
(*Heart of Roses, Friendship Heart*)

Heart Christening Robe
Judith Adams

Judith is a high school teacher living in Sydney, Australia with her husband Ross, an orthodontist, son Steven, daughter Catherine and dog Ixie. She is a graduate of the University of Sydney with a science degree majoring in pure mathematics and postgraduate education qualifications.

Judith has been smocking since 1984 She calls it her 'portable passion' and fits teaching and designing around her children's busy ice and inline hockey schedules. She specialises in smocking on embroidered English netting and developed the technique of layering the netting over silk organza to produce plump pleats worthy of the time spent smocking over them. The smocked embroidered netting creates wonderful christening robes, collars and delightful sewing accessories, all with a luxurious and opulent appearance. The Status Thimble, her mail order business, was born from the desire of others who love the embroidered English netting and had little access to it.

Travelling to the United States to teach during their spring and autumn each year allows Judith to meet hundreds of fellow smockers as passionate about their needlework as she is, and also gives her the opportunity to source new treats for her customers. She is a regular attendee at the annual Smocking Arts Guild of America National Convention, and has been honoured to teach there in 1999, 2000 and 2002.

Contributing to *Embroidery from the Heart* had a special meaning for Judith, as her father died of a massive heart attack and she wanted to support such a worthwhile cause.

Judith designed a beautiful hand-smocked christening gown with heirloom hearts. 'I designed the gown because I believe it touches the hearts of all who see a small baby in a wonderful dress. There is also that precious link between young and old.'

Judith may be contacted at: 11 Leatherwood Court, Baulkham Hills NSW 2153, phone/fax (02) 9686 2713 e-mail: adams@mt.net.au

Smocking stitches used: Cable stitch, four-cable beaded flower, one-step half space wave, one-step wave, outline stitch.

Embroidery stitches used: Lazy daisy stitch, wound ribbon rose.

MATERIALS REQUIRED

basic square yoke baby dress pattern, size 3 to 6
     months
2 ½ yd (2.25 m) ivory silk dupion, 45 inches (115 cm)
     wide
20 inches (50 cm) ivory baby entredeux
20 inches (50 cm) French lace edging 18 mm wide
7 yd (6.5 m) French lace edging 1 ¼ inch (4 cm) wide
8 ¼ yd (7.5 m) French lace insertion ¾ inch (18 mm)
     wide
1 packet Mill Hill Antique Seed Beads, Royal Pearl
     No. 03021
2 cards Cascade House Stranded Silk 1000 (ivory)
2 yd (2 m) ivory silk ribbon 2 mm wide
1 ¾ yd (1.5 m) double-faced 3 mm antique white satin
     ribbon
needles:
     #7 and #9 darners
     #20 chenille
12 inches (30 cm) fine piping cord
1 spool Mettler 60/2 machine embroidery cotton 703
     (ivory)
2 small mother-of-pearl buttons
fading marking pen
fine glass-headed pins
smocking pleater and spool of contrasting machine
     thread for pleating

Preparation

This christening robe has been designed to fit a child 3 to 6 months in age.

Use the front and back yoke pattern pieces from the commercial pattern. Square off the bottom of the sleeve pattern piece, ensuring that the end of the short sleeve is approximately 6 cm from the underarm seam. Create a new front yoke lining pattern using the front yoke pattern piece and the front armhole cutting guide, extending it 4 ¼ inches (11 cm) past the bottom of the original front yoke. This lining will extend behind the smocking, hiding the thread tails and make the gown more comfortable to wear.

Make sure that all pattern pieces are cut along the lengthwise grain of the fabric so that the slubs in the silk run parallel to the hemline.

From the silk dupion, cut out the front and back skirts, making the pieces 34 inches (85 cm) long by the full width of the fabric. Mark and cut out the armholes on the back skirt only, not the front skirt. Cut out one front yoke, one extended front yoke lining, four back yokes, two sleeves and a placket measuring 1 ½ x 10 inches (4 x 25 cm). On the crosswise grain cut a binding for the piping measuring 1 ½ x 12 inches (4 x 30 cm).

Pleating

Prepare the smocking pleater with needles to pleat 12 full-space rows and including as many half-space rows as possible. Pleat these 12 rows across the full width of the fabric, positioning Row 1, ⅜ inch (1 cm) in from the raw edge. Ensure that the pleater threads are longer than the width of the silk, as you may wish to spread out the fabric to attach the shaped lace before working the smocking. It is a matter of ease and preference as to whether the gown is smocked and then the lace shaping added, or the lace attached to the front only and then smocked. I prefer to attach the lace first, although it can be a little fiddley working with it in position.

There will be one holding row at the top of the skirt and none at the bottom. Do not cut out any armhole marking.

When pleating silk dupion, use the 'pleat and steam' method, steaming the fabric on the pleater needles at every turn of the pleater handle. Clear the fabric from the needles and keep repeating the steaming process until the whole piece is pleated. You do not need to wait for each small section to dry. Leave the pleating threads long and tie into one big bunch at each end.

Prepare the two sleeves by using the heirloom technique of a 'roll and whip' seam to attach the wide edging to the bottom of each sleeve. Thread the pleater to pleat three half-space rows through the silk sleeve. Position the sleeve so the lace seam will run through an empty needle space to the right of the third pleater needle, and again use the 'pleat and steam' method. There are no extra holding rows on the sleeves.

If you do not have access to a pleater many fine needlework stores offer a mail order pleating service, charging per row of gathering.

The geometric smocking is worked in 3 strands of silk using the #9 darner; the picture-smocked hearts are worked in 4 strands using the #7 darner.

Pleating

Sleeves

The graph for the sleeve (diagram 1) shows a one-step full space wave with beaded cables at the top and bottom of each wave. To stitch a beaded cable, simply take a stitch through the first pleat of the cable, slide the bead onto the needle and stitch through the second pleat to complete the beaded cable.

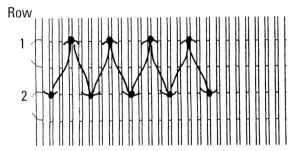

Diagram 1: Sleeve smocking pattern

Begin with a beaded up cable on the top pleating thread, Row 1, followed by a one-step wave to Row 2, the third pleating thread, and then a beaded down cable. The gathering thread in the centre of the group of three will simply hold the pleats together nicely but will not be used as a stitching line.

Skirt

In order to centre the design on the skirt (see diagram 2), the smocking will be worked, for the first row only, from the centre two pleats to the left using just half of a long piece of thread. When the left-hand side of the panel is finished, the pleated skirt will be turned upside down, the needle threaded with the remainder of the long thread and smocked to complete the row.

To begin, find the centre two pleats and cut a piece of silk thread twice the normal length of 20 inches (50 cm), placing 3 strands in the #9 darner. Follow the graph carefully and begin with the second row of smocking, stitching a down cable on Row 3 over the centre two pleats. Work this cable using thread from the centre of the long piece. This

means a large tail of thread will lie on the pleats to the right of the first cable stitch.

Continue by working an up cable, then a one-step half space wave to Row 3 ½, then stitch a down cable followed by an up cable. Smock another one-step half space wave to Row 4 and stitch a beaded down cable. Move up to Row 3 ½ and work an up cable, then a down cable. Continue up to Row 3 and smock three cables, up, down, up, before returning to Row 3 ½. Remember to always stitch a single beaded cable on Row 4. Do not end off this row of smocking until you have completed the other side and have checked that the two sides of the design are symmetrical and that you have left at least a full seam allowance.

Return to the centre and thread the needle with the long tail left hanging on the front. Turn the pleated silk upside down to smock back the other way and turn the graph upside down so that the correct stitches will be worked. After completing the smocking of this row, check both final stitches for symmetry and end off with a knot on the back. Mark your graph to indicate where your stitches will begin on the left-hand side and work all following rows from left to right.

Left-handed smockers will naturally work all rows from right to left.

Begin the smocking between Rows 2 and 3 using the same stitch as the row below. To work the beaded flowers on Row 2 at the peak of each wave, start with a beaded up cable. Position the needle to complete stitching a beaded down cable—however, slide the needle through two pleats to emerge in the valley above the beaded up cable. Slide a bead on the needle and stitch a beaded up cable, using the same pleats as the beaded down cable below it. Finish off with another beaded up cable. Continue smocking with the one-step wave to Row 2 ½.

The mirror image of these two rows is worked from Row 10 to Row 12.

Turn the smocking over to reveal the back of the work and using 2 strands of silk thread, backsmock in cable stitch across Rows 4, 5, 6, 7, 8, 9 and 10, then backsmock in outline stitch across Row 1 ½. This will hold the pleats together before stitching the hearts on the front.

Draw a heart on a piece of stiff paper that measures between 1 ½–1 ¾ inches (4–4.5 cm) in length, making it plump and rounded. Fold the paper in half to check the two sides are the same,

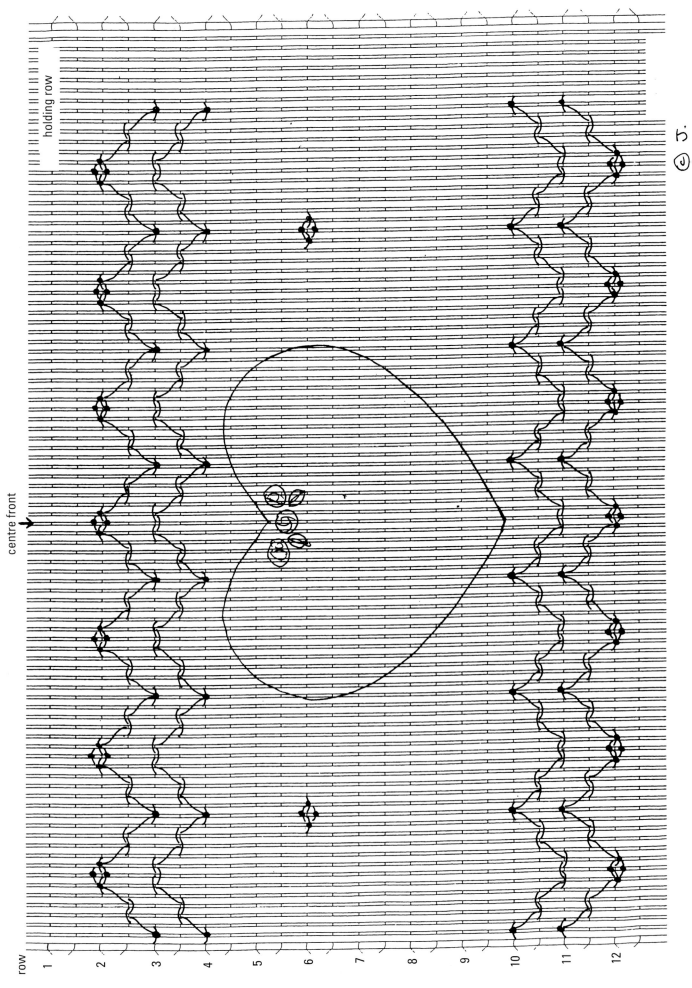

Diagram 2: Skirt smocking pattern with beaded embroidered heart

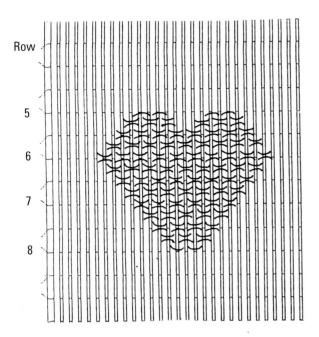

Diagram 3: Picture smocked heart

down cable followed by a beaded up cable. Work the next stitch as a beaded down cable, completing the cable by pushing the needle back through three pleats to emerge in the valley underneath the first beaded down cable. Finish the flower with a beaded down cable and end off on the back. Once the smocking is completed, block the panel to set the pleats to the correct size.

**Diagram 4
Four-cable beaded flower**

Step 1

Step 2

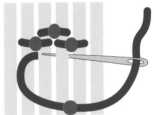

then cut out. Place this template in the centre of the smocking and trace around it. Smock over the tracing in outline stitch, then work around the outside of the shape, beading each outline stitch.

The two picture-smocked hearts (diagram 3) each cover 20 pleats. Smock each row, turning the fabric to work the next row back the other way. Make sure the rows of cable stitch contain plump stitches with a down cable stacked on an up cable.

Using 4 strands of silk thread in the #7 darner, count 20 pleats to the right of the beaded heart along Row 6 and begin the bottom of the picture-smocked heart on pleat 21. Follow the graph carefully and smock 19 cable stitches, starting with a down cable. Turn the work upside down and move in one pleat, then smock back the other way, with 17 cable stitches. Continue following the graph until there are only five cables on the bottom of the heart. Return to the top of the heart with a new thread and stack 19 cables, then 17 back the other way. The next line will have 7 cables smocked, before skipping one cable to leave a gap and smocking a further 7 cables. Finish the heart with 5 cables stacked over the top of each side of the heart.

Work the second heart in a similar manner.

Thread 2 strands into the #9 darner and work the beaded flowers (diagram 4) between the beaded heart and the picture-smocked hearts. Each flower covers 4 pleats and begins with a beaded

Embroidery

Inside the beaded heart (diagram 2) are three wound ribbon roses and two lazy daisy stitch leaves, all worked in 2 mm ivory silk ribbon. Begin the ribbon roses with a small five-spoked wheel worked in 1 strand of the silk embroidery thread. Weave the silk ribbon over and under the spokes, around the wheel, to create each rose. Using the #20 chenille needle, add the two silk ribbon lazy daisy leaves to complete the floral spray.

Blocking the smocking

Use the front yoke lining pattern piece as a blocking guide and pin the smocked panel onto the ironing board, easing out the smocking to reach from side seam to side seam. Adjust the pleats on the gathering threads so that they are evenly spaced and vertical, then steam for about 2 or 3 minutes, from about 1 ½ inches (4 cm) above the smocking. *Never* touch smocking with the iron, now or later. Leave to dry, then remove all the gathering threads with the exception of the top two, which should be tied off to the correct width for the yoke so that the panel will not stretch with handling.

Lace shaping

The 18 mm insertion lace is shaped into one large heart and seven small hearts, each separated by a scallop (see diagram 5). There are three small hearts across the back, two small and one large on the front, and a small heart straddling each side seam. Using the lace shaping guides (templates A, B and C), trace the design onto tissue paper or Vilene. You may like to extend it to have the entire design on the one tracing. This will save you having to shape the lace in sections and unpin the shaped lace to reuse the guide.

The lace can easily be pinned to the guide on the ironing board, using the fine glass-headed pins. Push each pin into the lace on a very acute angle so that you can safely press over them without damage to either the pins or the iron.

Shape the lace on the guide, pinning every ½ inch (1 cm) on both sides of the lace and pulling the loopy outermost thread in the lace heading to curve the lace around the scallops and hearts. Pin the mitres at the top of each scallop and in each heart. Press the shaped lace on the guide, making sure that the iron is not too hot (just before Cotton is best), and that the pins do not enter the steam holes.

Remove the pins shaping the lace, and pin the lace where it crosses over at the base of each heart to keep the shape, plus the mitres on each heart and scallop. Stitch the mitres and trim away the excess lace.

The shaped lace may be hand-basted to the front only at this point, and to the remainder of the skirt later during construction. As the shaped lace should appear continuous around the skirt it will have to be joined together into a circle, and this is best done at the base of a small heart somewhere on the back or side of the gown. Position the shaped lace with the large lace heart in the centre of the front skirt, about 1 ¼ inches (3 cm) above the bottom. Pin in place, press, then hand-baste the shaped lace to the skirt using the machine thread.

Construction

After the gown has been smocked and the lace shaped, follow the instructions on the commercial pattern to construct the gown. All seams can be either French seams, or straight-stitched seams neatened with a zigzag or overlocking.

Draw the armhole curves on the front skirt but do not cut them out. Make a 5 inch (12 cm) slit down the centre of the back skirt and attach the placket. Using two rows of long machine stitches, gather the sleeve heads on the two sleeves, and also gather the back skirt either side of the placket. Neaten the bottom of the front yoke lining with a small hem or add some narrow lace, then join the front yoke lining to the back yoke linings at the shoulder seams. Also stitch the shoulder seams to join the front and back yokes, then construct the piping using the fine piping cord and the strip of silk.

Once the smocking has been blocked and the gathering threads, except the top two, removed, the piping can be attached. Position the piping to sit just above the top bead on the flowers along Row 2, then baste and stitch in place. Carefully place the front yoke on top and ensure it is centred with the smocking design before stitching through the piping and skirt.

The finished length of the shaped lace hearts design needs to be the same as the width of the finished skirt. Measure both, and adjust if necessary by trimming equal amounts from both

Diagram 5: Lace shaping pattern

sides of the back skirt to ensure it is the same finished size as the lace work. Remember to factor in the seam allowances on the side seams.

Attach the back skirt to the back yoke, then baste the entredeux along the complete neckline. Clip the entredeux batiste to allow it to sit flat and trim away the two ends of the entredeux just before the back seam of the back yoke. Pin the yoke linings over the yoke, right sides together, and stitch the keyhole, working up the back seam of one back yoke, around the neck and down the back seam of the other back yoke. Trim and neaten the seams, cutting the neckline seam allowance almost away. Machine or hand-stitch the back yoke lining to the back yoke where it joins the back skirt.

Attach the sleeves to the armholes and then join the side seams. Complete the neckline by cutting away the batiste on the side of the entredeux, then gathering the narrow lace edging and hand-stitching it to the entredeux. Attach the two small mother-of-pearl buttons to one side of the back closing and work the buttonholes.

Finish pinning and basting the shaped lace hearts in place over the side seams and joining at the rear.

The lace needs to be attached to the skirt with a very close zigzag very similar to a satin stitch, that is, just wide enough to cover the lace heading. On many machines you can use a stitch length of around 0.8 and a width of around 3. Work slowly, turning the fabric frequently to achieve a smooth edge on the shaped lace. Stitch the upper edge of the lace along the bottom scallops to the fabric, plus both sides of the lace of each heart shape. Do not stitch across the lace where it overlaps at the base of each heart. This will be done later.

Very carefully cut the fabric from behind the lace, all around the complete skirt, then zigzag the lace heading where the lace crosses over at the base of each heart. Trim away the bottom layer of this crossover lace.

Join the remaining 1 ½ inch (4 cm) French lace edging into a circle. Gather the lace by pulling the loopy thread on the top and distribute evenly around the scalloped lace hem, making sure you bulk a few extra gathers into the peaks of the scallops, and stitch to the shaped insertion.

Your wonderful heart christening gown is now ready to become a gift from the heart to a very precious little babe!

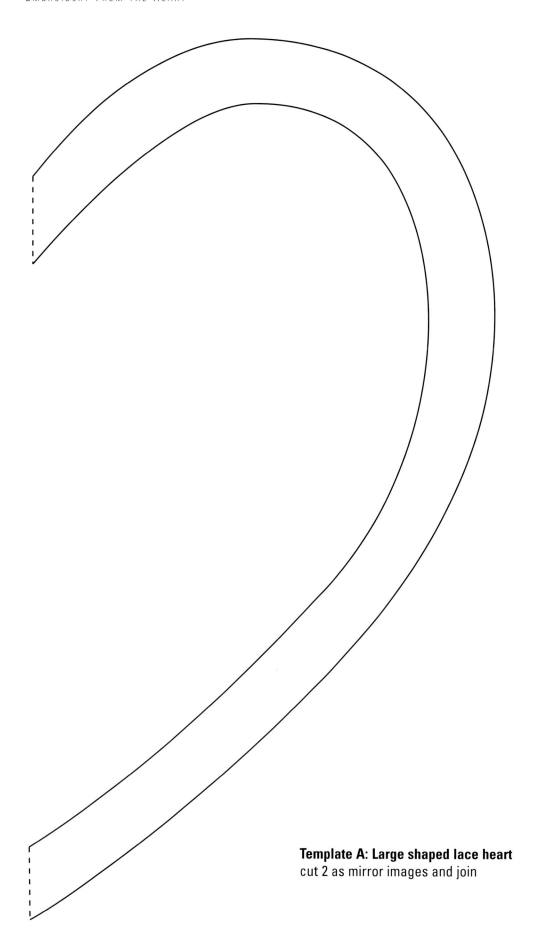

Template A: Large shaped lace heart
cut 2 as mirror images and join

Template B: Small shaped lace heart

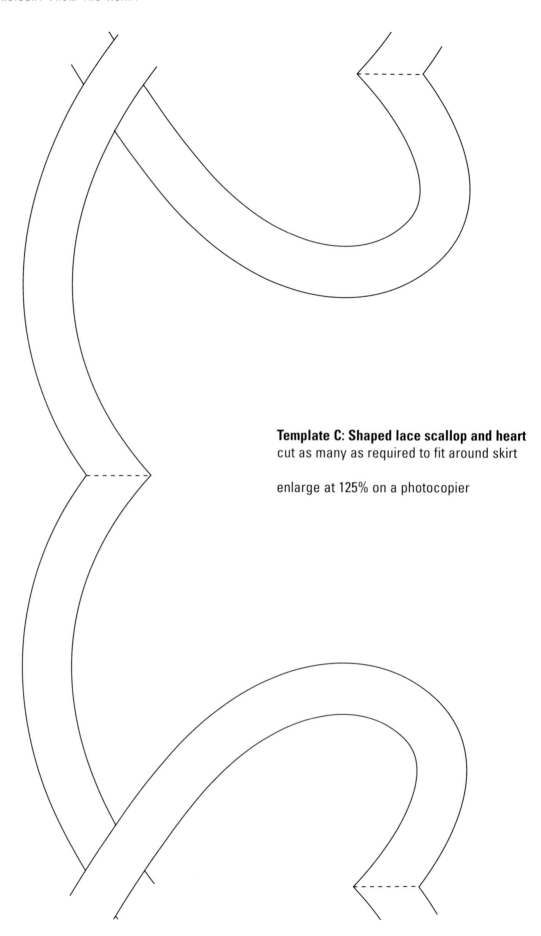

Template C: Shaped lace scallop and heart
cut as many as required to fit around skirt

enlarge at 125% on a photocopier

Heart of Roses
Margot Hammonds

Originally trained as an artist, Margot began embroidering five years ago. She enjoys working with beautiful materials, colours and textures, seeing embroidery as a delightfully tactile form of painting, and placing a strong emphasis on design techniques. She sometimes views her designs as more collage than embroidery.

Margot teaches regular classes in her studio in Mornington, Victoria and frequently travels to country areas and interstate to teach. She enjoys motivating her students and encouraging them to enjoy their creativity, and is particularly rewarded by their sense of accomplishment as they complete their projects.

Margot was inspired in this design for *Embroidery from the Heart* by one of her close friends, a nurse who provided her with information and drawings showing how the heart functions. Margot wanted to celebrate the wonder of the design of the heart and created a collection of silk roses representing a physical heart. 'My design is modelled on a heart, with the aorta and veins as rosebuds and leaves angled as our hearts lie within us.' It is a dimensional piece bursting out of its boundaries. Some of the silk ribbons used in the design were specially dyed to represent the different types of blood going in and out of the heart.

For Margot the project was a challenge; 'it is a privilege to create a piece to be used and enjoyed for such a purpose. A rose seems to be linked with the heart—the romantic, emotional, expansive nature of a person. A whiff of the perfume of a rose immediately lifts and warms me—maybe it touches others too!'

Margot may be contacted at: 47 Separation Street, Mornington Vic 3931,
phone/fax (03) 5975 1148
www.margothammonds.com.au
e-mail: margot@margothammonds.com.au

'Heart of Roses' is assembled on a background of painted leaves. The 'aorta' is indicated with leaves and buds with three embroidered buds as 'arteries'.

Stitches used: Apart from ribbon stitch and whipped running stitch, no specific embroidery stitches are required for this piece.

Note: Where the silk ribbons specified are not readily available you can substitute other brands using the photograph as a colour guide.

MATERIALS REQUIRED

7 mm silk ribbon:
3 ⅓ yd (3 m) Kacoonda 306 Olive Green
1 yd (1 m) Kacoonda 106 Antique Gold
13 mm silk ribbon:
2 ¼ yd (2 m) Kacoonda Waratah
1 yd (1 m) Kacoonda Berries
2 ¼ yd (2 m) Kacoonda 306 Olive Green
15 mm soft satin ribbon:
5 ½ yd (5 m) Margot's Leaves
25 mm wire-edged ribbon:
5 ½ yd (5 m) ET Diffusion Royal Brown
5 ½ yd (5 m) ET Diffusion Bronze Green
1 yd (1 m) Mokuba Organdy #14
1 yd (1 m) Mokuba Organdy #15
32 mm edge-dyed silk ribbon:
6 ⅔ yd (6 m) Margot's Ruby Port
Kacoonda Twist Thread 306 Olive Green
stamens
10 inch (25 cm) square of calico on which to construct the roses
16 x 18 inch (40 x 45 cm) furnishing weight moiré or jacquard
cottons to match colour of ribbons
glue stick
toothpicks
2 cotton wool balls
9 and 12 inch (23 and 30 cm) embroidery hoops
needles:
#9 crewel
#14, #18, #20 chenille
#4crewel embroidery
water-erasable pen
fabric paints of your choice, used to manufacturer's instructions

Preparation
Paint the underlying design of leaves onto the background fabric, using the pattern diagram as a guide.

Make up the three roses, the large buds and large leaves, which will be fixed onto the square of calico before being attached to the background fabric in the centre of the painted heart shape. No calico should be visible in the finished work. The small buds are embroidered directly onto the background fabric as pictured.

Full-blown rose
Cut the 32 mm silk into 20 petals: 5 x 2 ¾ inch (7 cm), 5 x 3 ⅛ inch (8 cm) and 10 x 3 ½ inch (9 cm).

Choose the shading of your flower by gathering one edge; the ungathered side is the dominating colour, so keep in mind which side to stitch. The same ribbon can be used to create two different coloured roses by reversing the side you gather.

Make up all the petals as follows:

Smear the glue stick on top corners and roll with a toothpick firmly on a 45-degree angle down towards centre. (See diagram 1.) With matching sewing cotton sew a small running stitch along base, easing gently to a curve and knot. Keep the sizes separate.

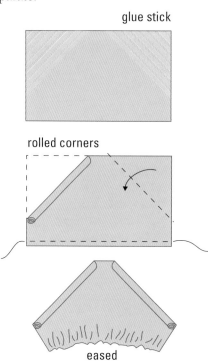

Diagram 1: Petals

a 'vena cava' could be added for more realism

darkest rose

open rose lighter colour

light colour

soft bud

'artery'

Pattern and tracing diagram

When all petals are made, construct the rose on a piece of calico stretched over a hoop. Draw a circle ¾ inch (2 cm) in diameter, make 5 divisions. Place the centres of the 2 ¾ inch (7 cm) petals at each numbered point and stitch securely, with the rolled edge to the outside. Have all petals pointing around the same way (like a windmill). Take one inside point of a petal, and sew the tip into the space between the next petal and the one after, turning the point so that the edges face outward. (See diagram 2.)

Continue to stitch each petal down until the fifth petal, which passes underneath the first petal to be attached. A simple slogan to understand where to sew is 'go past the neighbour and park next door!'

Catch the other 'outer' corner close to petals in the calico. Let it be fairly 'soft' if an open look is required. Pull tighter to 'close' the centre more. Spread the centre apart to place stamens. Knot two lots of 5 stamens and place crosswise in the centre. Stitch into place and cover stitches and knots with a cross-stitch of 7 mm Antique Gold silk ribbon. Fill in any space between stamens and petals with silk knots with knots of the same ribbon. (See diagram 3.)

Diagram 3

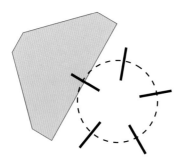

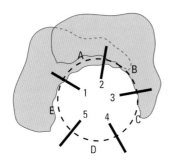

Diagram 2 Full-blown rose
place centre of petals on each mark, folds facing down
place end of petal 1 to point B, between 2 and 3; petal 2 to point C, and so on

Apply next round of petals in the spaces of the first. Stitch onto the calico and keep the rolled edge on the outside. Continue with the outside layers of petals, building up more on one side than the other to give a 'tilt' to the rose. The closer you place the petals, the 'tighter' your rose will be.

Continue to attach the petals around until you have the desired size of rose.

Rose with wound centre

The second rose has a wound centre, which is then surrounded by petals. Cut a piece of 32 mm ribbon 8 inches (20 cm) long. Fold the cut end to the selvedge, roll up the corner until a straight roll is vertical to edge of ribbon. Secure and lightly gather and attach the rest of the length. (See diagram 4.) Place this rolled centre onto the calico and firmly attach with stitches around the base, letting it stand up straight.

Make 16 petals: Cut 5 x 2 ¾ inch (7 cm), 5 x 3 ⅛ inch (8 cm) and 6 x 3 ½ inch (9 cm).

Place the five 2 ¾ inch (7 cm) petals equally around the centre, and the five 3 ⅛ inch (8 cm)

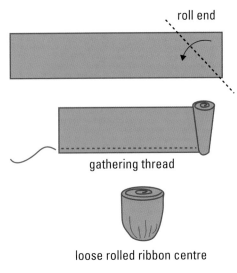

roll end

gathering thread

loose rolled ribbon centre

Diagram 4

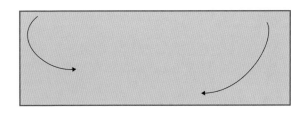

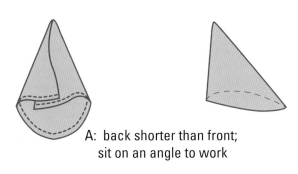

A: back shorter than front;
sit on an angle to work

1st   2nd

B: add petals at the side

petals in the spaces around the outside of the first, overlapping by half. Allow to 'breathe' by letting a little space between the 'layers'. Again you may like to 'tilt' the rose by placing more towards the front of the flower. Add the third layer similarly.

Make a second rose in the same way, reversing the colour if you wish.

Soft bud

Make a cone of 4 inches (10 cm), and 4 petals: 2 x 2 ½ inch (6 cm) and 2 x 2 ¾ inch (7 cm). (See diagram 5.) Make the 2 ½ inch (6 cm) petals rolled so that the top edge is almost meeting; apply these around bud, then add the 2 ¾ inch (7 cm) petals to balance. (See diagram 5B.)

Medium wound buds

Make three buds with one rolled petal and one surrounding. (See diagram 6.)

Leaves

Make up six leaves in the ET Diffusion 25 mm wire-edged ribbons, three in each colour. Make up four leaves in the 15 mm satin ribbon. (See diagram 7.)

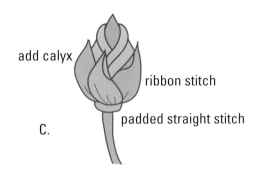

add calyx

ribbon stitch

padded straight stitch

C.

Diagram 5: Bud—cone and petals

Assembly and finishing

Place the roses on their calico base within the painted heart, facing outward. Place the large soft bud at point of heart and attach last petal. Use 13 mm silk to make the calyx of three ribbon stitches. (See diagram 5C.)

Place the three medium wound buds between the roses and securely stitch. You might like to

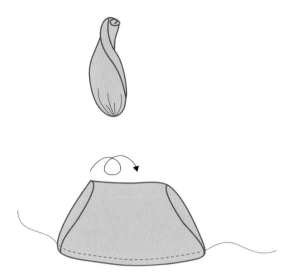

roll one side; gather base of other side;
catch at base of bud with tiny stitch

Diagram 6: Rolled bud

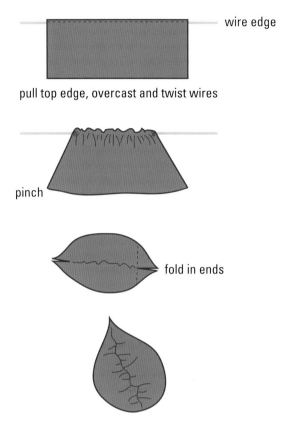

wire edge

pull top edge, overcast and twist wires

pinch

fold in ends

Diagram 7: Leaves

work ribbon stitch petals in 32 mm Ruby Port silk ribbon to 'expand' the buds.

Place the wire-edged leaves around the heart. On the 'aorta' line work four small buds in ribbon stitch in matching colours in 7 mm or 13 mm ribbon. The larger buds have a small wound centre to give them volume (refer to finished piece). Give each a ribbon stitch calyx embroidered in olive green ribbon, and embroider three more ribbon stitch buds and 13 mm silk leaves. Add the organza leaves and the 7 mm silk ribbon leaves.

Make stems of whipped running stitch in olive green double twist silk (Kacoonda 306) for the 'artery' of flowers. Embroider three large soft buds in ribbon stitch in 13 mm silk ribbon in burgundy Waratah ribbon. Give each a ribbon stitch calyx in 7 mm olive green silk ribbon and a leaf or two in the same ribbon in ribbon stitch.

Have your finished work professionally mounted.

Evening Bag
Susan O'Connor

Susan has always had a passion for textiles and embroidery, and first learned basic embroidery stitches as a child. Since then she has expanded her knowledge and now uses a diverse range of techniques in her work.

Susan is trained as a secondary Art and Craft teacher, and teaches both in Australia and overseas. She finds few things more satisfying than sharing the pleasure of embroidery with others. Susan is also the editor of *Australian Smocking and Embroidery* and editor-at-large of *Inspirations* magazine.

For *Embroidery from the Heart* Susan has created an embroidered evening bag using furnishing fabrics embellished with silk embroidery and beading. She believes 'a bag is a container. It is useful as well as decorative. In a container we can hold things—just like a heart.'

Susan may be contacted by e-mail at: susan@psoc.com.au

This delightful bag is created from a selection of silk fabrics that I have collected over the years. You may choose to use similar fabrics, or put together a slightly different collection.

Stitches used: Back stitch, blanket stitch, bullion knot, bullion loop, detached chain stitch, fly stitch, French knot, long stitch, satin stitch, short stitch, stem stitch, straight stitch, twisted chain stitch.

MATERIALS REQUIRED

8 x 24 in (20 x 60 cm) green silk jacquard for sides, handle and 5th stripe
4 x 24 in (10 x 60 cm) red silk for handle lining
small amounts of 7 silk fabrics to make up the panels that form the front and back of the bag
12 x 24 in (30 x 60 cm) silk lining
4 in (10 cm) old gold cord for clasp
white pearl button (2 holes)
14 red glass hearts
1 packet red seed beads
24 in (60 cm) red mini piping
Madeira stranded silk:
    #0105, 0113, 0210, 0701, 0713, 0803, 0806,
    0811, 0812, 0813, 0815, 0901, 0903, 1407,
    1408, 1603, 2208, 2209
machine sewing thread
needles:
    #10 straw
    #10 crewel
    beading needle
small piece applique paper (Vliesofix)
soft lead pencil
white tissue paper and pencil
4 in (10 cm) embroidery hoop

Cutting out

All dimensions for pattern pieces include a ⅜ in (1 cm) seam allowance.

Front and back Cut 2 strips of each of the following fabrics (one each for front and back):
Strip 1: 1 ¼ x 7 in (3 x 18 cm) pale pink
Strip 2: 1 ¼ x 7 in (3 x 18 cm) sage
Strip 3: 1 ¼ x 7 in (3 x 18 cm) butter
Strip 4: 1 ¼ x 7 in (3 x 18 cm) cream
Strip 5: 1 ⅝ x 7 in (4 x 18 cm) deep red
Strip 6: 2 ¼ x 7 in (5.5 x 18 cm) green
Strip 7: 1 ½ x 7 in (3.5 x 18 cm) coral
Strip 8: 1 ¾ x 7 in (4.5 x 18 cm) dusty pink

Strip 9: 1 ¼ x 7 in (3 x 18 cm) sage
Strip 10: 1 ⅝ x 7 in (4 x 18 cm) butter

Sides: Cut 1 strip green silk measuring 2 ¼ x 21 in (5.5 x 53 cm).

Handles: Cut 2 strips green silk measuring 1 ⅝ x 13 in (4 x 33 cm).

Handle lining: Cut 2 strips red silk measuring 1 ⅝ x 13 in (4 x 33 cm).

Front and back panel lining: Cut 2 pieces silk lining measuring 7 ¼ x 7 in (18.5 x 18 cm).

Side lining: Cut a strip of silk lining measuring 2 ¼ x 21 in (5.5 x 53 cm).

Machine-stitch 10 strips together to make the front panel, following the numerical order. Do the same for the back panel. Trim and press the seams open flat.

Transferring the design

With a soft pencil, trace the embroidery pattern onto white tissue paper, marking the position of the seams and the placement of the flowers for rows 2, 4, 9 and 10. Trace the complete embroidery design for rows 5, 6, 7 and 8. Pin the pattern securely into position on the right side of the front panel, ensuring that the seams match their corresponding markings. Using contrasting machine thread, tailor's tack the position of the flowers in rows 2, 4, 9 and 10, and tack the outlines of the design of rows 5, 6, 7 and 8 with tiny stitches. Dampen the tissue paper with a sponge, allow it to soften and gently remove, leaving the stitched outline of the design.

Embroidery

Work the embroidery on the front panel before you make up the bag.

All embroidery is worked in 2 strands of thread unless otherwise specified. Use the #10 straw needle for all French knots and bullions, the #10 crewel needle for all other stitches.

You will need the embroidery hoop to work sections of the embroidery in strips 5, 6 and 8.

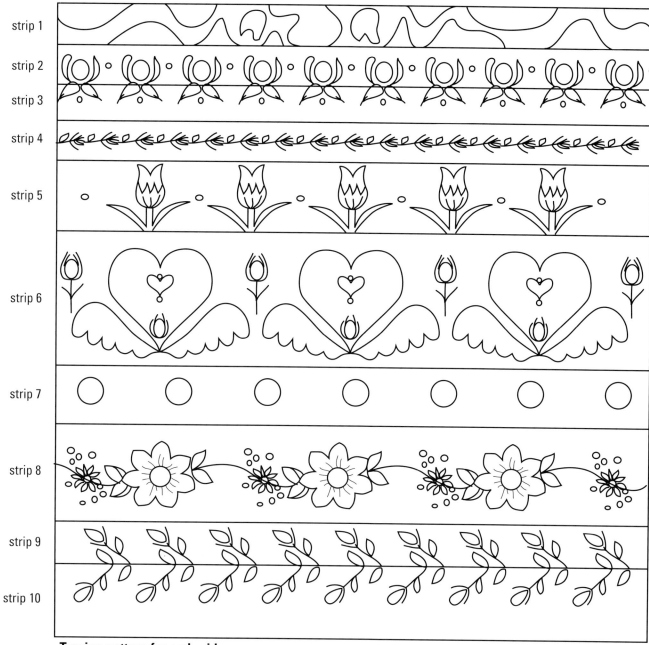

strip 1
strip 2
strip 3
strip 4
strip 5
strip 6
strip 7
strip 8
strip 9
strip 10

Tracing pattern for embroidery

Strip 1

Using Madeira 0803, outline the jacquard patterns in the fabric with twisted chain stitch.

Strips 2 and 3

Following the pattern and diagram 1, embroider the rose centres with Madeira 0812 in 10-wrap bullions. Work the rose outers, making three 10-wrap bullions in Madeira 0813 and three 10-wrap bullions in Madeira 8015. Following diagram 2, using Madeira 1603 work fly-stitch sepals and detached chain leaves. Work French knots in Madeira 1603 between each of the roses on strip 2 and between the leaves on strip 3.

centre bullion, 10 wraps

Diagram 1

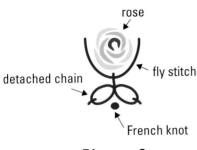

Diagram 2

Strip 4

Using Madeira 1408, work stem stitch along the top and bottom seams of the strip.

Work a row of basting in a single strand of Madeira 2208 just inside each of the rows of stem stitch.

Following the pattern and diagram 3, using a single strand of Madeira 1713, work 17 straight-stitch flowers in the centre of the strip (5 straight stitches per flower). Add a fly-stitch sepal to each flower with a single strand of Madeira 1408, connecting it to the preceding flower to make a vine. Work a detached chain leaf to the upper side of each fly-stitch stem with a single strand of Madeira 1408.

Diagram 3

Strip 5

Place the fabric into the small embroidery hoop and move it along as you work each tulip, following the pattern and diagram 4. Using 1 strand of Madeira 0113, follow the tacked outline, beginning at the base of each tulip. Working long and short stitches, blend into Madeira 0105 one-third of the way up for the top two-thirds of the flower. Work 4 or 5 straight stitches radiating from the base of the flower in 1 strand of Madeira 2209.

Work back stitch around the lower third of the tulip in 1 strand of Madeira 2209. Work the stem in 1 strand of Madeira 1408 in satin stitch, and the leaves in long and short stitch in 1 strand of the same thread.

Work a French knot between each flower in Madeira 2209 and a line of stem stitch along the seam between strips 5 and 6 in the same thread.

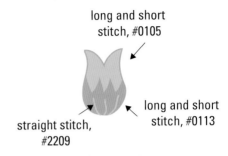

Diagram 4

Strip 6

Trace three hearts from diagram 5 onto the appliqué paper. Fuse the paper to the wrong side of a small piece of red silk. Cut out the hearts, remove the backing paper and fuse them onto the fabric of strip 6 in the correct position.

Using 1 strand of Madeira 0105, work around the hearts in small, even blanket stitches.

Diagram 5
Heart template for strip 6

Place the work in the hoop to work the first set of wings, moving it along for each set.

With 1 strand of Madeira 2209, fill the wings in satin stitch and work back stitch around them.

Work the seven roses, beginning with a 10-wrap bullion in Madeira 0811 for the centre, and working three 10-wrap bullion petals in 1 strand of Madeira 0210. Work two fly-stitch sepals in 1 strand of Madeira 1407.

Diagram 6

10-wrap bullion

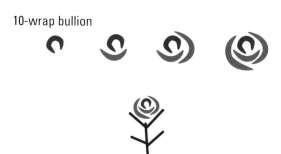

On each of the four roses outside the hearts, work a stem in back stitch and a straight-stitch leaf either side of the stem with 1 strand of Madeira 1407.

Strip 7

Work a line of stem stitch in Madeira 0812 along the seams between strips 6 and 7 and strips 7 and 8.

Work the circles in satin stitch in 1 strand of Madeira 2209. Back-stitch around the circles in the same thread.

Diagram 7

Strip 8

Work the line of the vine in stem stitch in 1 strand of Madeira 1603. Work the daisies with 10 detached chain petals in 1 strand of Madeira 2208 and a French knot centre in Madeira 0812. Work scattered French knots around the daisies in Madeira 0806.

You will need to place your work in a hoop to embroider the large flowers, using 1 strand of Madeira 0901 in satin stitch radiating out from the centre, keeping your stitches outside the central circle. Work some straight-stitch highlights in 1 strand of Madeira 0903, also radiating out from the centre (3 or 4 per petal). Fill the central circle with French knots in 1 strand of Madeira 2208.

The leaves are worked in satin stitch with 1 strand of Madeira 1408.

Strips 9 and 10

Work the main stem along the seam between strips 9 and 10, and the flower stems, in stem stitch in Madeira 1408. In the same thread work the detached chain leaves. The flowers are embroidered in satin stitch in 1 strand of Madeira 0701 and highlighted with three straight stitches radiating out from the base of each flower in 1 strand Madeira 0210. Back-stitch around the flowers in 1 strand of Madeira 0210. Attach the flowers to the stem with fly stitch in 1 strand of Madeira 1408.

Construction

Stitch the green side panel to the embroidered front panel, lining them up at the top right side of the front panel with right sides together; stitch down the right side, along the bottom and up the left side. Attach the back panel to the side piece in the same way. Turn the bag right side out.

Diagram 8

front

Make up the lining using the same method, but leaving a 3 in (8 cm) opening in the front bottom seam (diagram 9).

Diagram 9

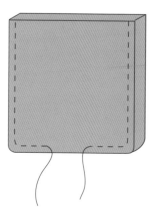

Make up the handles, laying one of each of the green and red silk handle pieces together with right sides facing, and stitch a seam along either side. Make the second handle in the same way. Turn them right side out and press.

Take the 4 in (10 cm) piece of old gold cord for the clasp, make a loop and pin and tack it into position, with the ends lining up with the top edge at the centre back of the bag (diagram 10).

Diagram 10

Attach the mini piping with the raw edge lining up with the upper edge of the bag and tack into place, overlapping the ends at the clasp at the centre back.

With right sides together, pin the two ends of one handle piece to the front of the bag in the desired position and tack into place. Repeat for the handle on the back of the bag (diagram 11).

Diagram 11

Keeping the lining inside out, slip it over the outer bag, lining up the top edges. Make sure the handles and clasp are hanging down inside the lining so as not to get caught up in the seam, and tack into position. Machine-stitch around the top of the bag, securing the lining to the outer (diagram 12).

Diagram 12

Using the opening left at the base of the lining, turn the bag right side out, slip-stitch the lining closed and work a few stitches to attach the lining to the outer along the inside bottom of the bag.

Beading

Refer to the photograph as a guide while you are working the beading.

Thread the beading needle with a single strand of Madeira 0210. Use a long enough strand of thread to bead across the bottom of the bag without having to rethread the needle. Secure with several small back stitches at the inside bottom of the bag. Bring the needle through the fabric at the seam between strips 9 and 10 on the right-hand side.

Slide 13 red seed beads onto the thread and lay the strand of beads along the seam, securing at the corner with a small stitch. Go back along the strand of beads and couch between every second bead to the seam. When you reach the first bead, take the needle along through all 13 beads again, bring it out at the end and slide 13 more seed beads onto the needle. Lay the strand along the bottom seam and secure one-fifth of the way along with a small stitch. Work your way back along the strand of beads, couching between every second bead until you get back to the corner, then take your needle back though the 13 beads.

Slide 13 more beads onto the needle and repeat the process. Continue this way across the bottom of the bag until you reach the left-hand corner, and then once more up the side to the seam between the ninth and tenth strips. Take the needle inside the bag and finish off firmly with several small back stitches.

Rethread the beading needle and bring it from the inside of the bag to the right-hand bottom corner. Thread a heart and a bead onto the needle, take the needle back through the heart and secure with a small stitch at the corner of the bag. Thread 13 seed beads onto the needle, a heart, a seed bead, then take the needle back through the heart and the 13th bead, thread 12 more beads onto the needle, pull the thread through firmly and secure to the lower seam of the bag one-fifth of the way along the seam just below where you secured the first 13 beads on the base row of beading (see diagram 13). Slide a bead, heart and bead onto the needle and take the needle back through the heart and bead again. Secure in the same place. Thread 13 more beads onto the needle, a heart, a bead, then take the needle back through the heart and the 13th bead, thread 12 more beads onto the needle, pull the thread through firmly and secure to the lower seam two-fifths of the way along.

Diagram 13

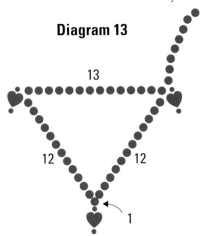

Continue in this way along the length of the bag. When you reach the left-hand corner, thread a heart and a bead onto the needle, take the needle back through the heart and secure at the corner, take the needle through to inside the bag and secure again.

To finish the hearts in strip 6, rethread the needle and bring it from inside the bag through to the top centre of the first heart. Thread a bead,

heart and bead onto the needle, then take the needle back through the heart and the first bead. Take the needle back through the fabric to inside the bag and finish off securely (diagram 14). Repeat this for the other two hearts, ensuring that the glass hearts lie flat when attached.

Diagram 14

Finishing off

Position the button on the centre front of the bag to correspond with the clasp, with the two holes vertical. Stitch it into position using 2 strands of Madeira 0210; before finishing off, bring the needle out through the top hole, through the last red glass heart and down through the bottom hole (see diagram 15), taking the thread to the back of the front panel and finishing off securely.

Diagram 15

Hearts and Butterfly
Gary Clarke

After completing formal art training Gary began his career in textile design working as a designer for Sheridan Australia in Hobart. He later moved into graphics and interior design before discovering needlework in 1990. Gary became interested in embroidery after teaching design techniques at a Launceston needlework store.

Today Gary is known as much for his dexterity with a needle and his ability to teach these skills as he is for design. He travels widely throughout Australia demonstrating his work and teaching embroidery and design. He writes frequently for embroidery publications and magazines and has also published five books which have been distributed around the world.

Gary believes that everyone is creative in some way and that creativity is a gift that should be explored and shared. His love of design is evident in his approach to his work: 'My philosophy is that embroidery is an art form no different than any other. One simply uses a needle and thread instead of a brush and paint.'

For *Embroidery from the Heart* Gary chose to create a silk thread embroidery on organza, free floating above a butterfly in the background, 'because of its fine and fragile nature'.

Gary may be contacted at: PO Box 787, Launceston Tas 7250, phone (03) 6334 1515, fax (03) 6334 1525 e-mail: stitching.heirloom@microtech.com.au

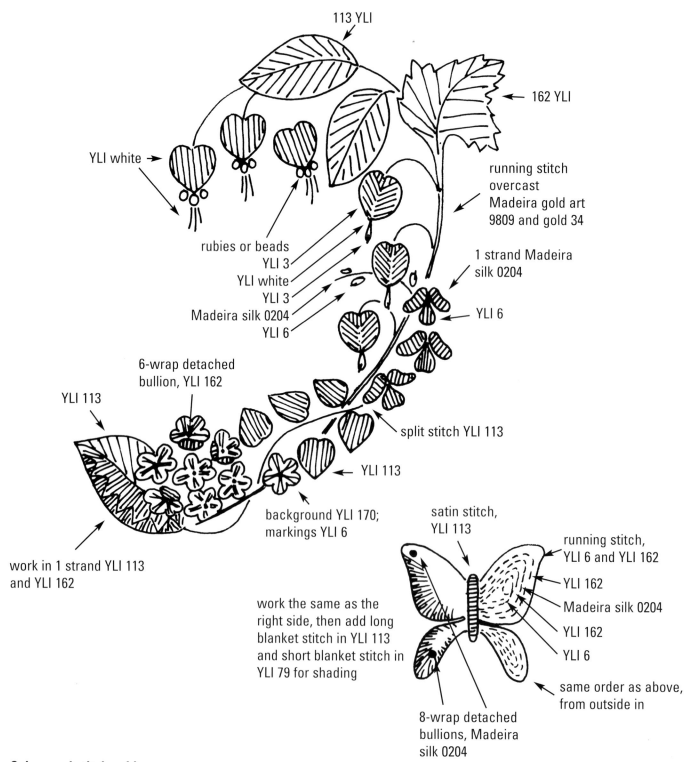

113 YLI

162 YLI

YLI white →

running stitch
overcast
Madeira gold art
9809 and gold 34

rubies or beads
YLI 3
YLI white
YLI 3
Madeira silk 0204
YLI 6

1 strand Madeira
silk 0204

YLI 6

6-wrap detached
bullion, YLI 162

YLI 113

split stitch YLI 113

YLI 113

background YLI 170;
markings YLI 6

work in 1 strand YLI 113
and YLI 162

satin stitch,
YLI 113

running stitch,
YLI 6 and YLI 162

YLI 162

Madeira silk 0204

YLI 162

YLI 6

work the same as the
right side, then add long
blanket stitch in YLI 113
and short blanket stitch in
YLI 79 for shading

same order as above,
from outside in

8-wrap detached
bullions, Madeira
silk 0204

Colour and stitch guide
work the satin stitch in the directions indicated. Work
with 2 strands of silk unless otherwise indicated.

Stitches used: Blanket stitch, couching, long and short blanket stitch, detached bullion stitch, running stitch, satin stitch, split stitch

MATERIALS REQUIRED

½ x 1 ¾ inch (1 x 4.5 cm) pine to make two frames
   approximately 17 inches (44 cm) square
white organza 20 inches (50 cm) square for
   embroidery
extra white organza for butterfly
YLI Silk Floss thread:
   white, 3, 6, 79, 113, 160, 162, 170
   Madeira Silk 0204
   Madeira gold 34, gold art 9809
9 rubies or beads

embroidery needle as fine as one is able to thread
white 10-sheet cardboard 17 inches (44 cm) square
foam core 17 inches (44 cm) square
PVA glue
masking tape
glue stick
small embroidery hoop
fine fuse wire

From the pine make two frames 17 inches (44 cm) square. Mitre the corners, using PVA glue and V staples or fine tacks to hold them firm. They have to be strong enough to resist the pull of the organza stretched over them.

Cutting guide for cardboard background

Organza embroidery

Fix the square of white organza over one of the frames. Starting at the top right-hand corner, staple the fabric to the frame, then stretch it diagonally to the bottom left corner and staple it there. Stretch the fabric evenly down the right side of the frame, stapling as you go, and work around the frame, stretching and stapling until the organza is as tight as a drum skin.

Trace the flower design outline onto transfer paper and transfer onto the organza with a soft lead black pencil.

Follow the detailed colour and stitch guide to embroider the organza.

Backing design

Mark out the backing design onto a piece of 10-sheet cardboard the same size as the second frame.

Fix the cutting design over the cardboard and, using a very sharp scalpel or fine craft knife, cut through the cardboard along the design lines. With your fingers gently push the card upwards along the inner curves of the cuts (see photograph for the effect required).

Using the glue stick, apply glue all over the back of the cardboard and fix it to a piece of foam core the size of the frame.

Staple the foam core to the second frame.

Butterfly

Tightly stretch the small piece of organza in a small embroidery hoop. Mould the fuse wire to the shape of the butterfly and lay the shape on the organza. Couch the wire to the organza, then embroider the design following the colour and stitch guide.

Carefully cut out the butterfly.

Assembling

Glue the butterfly to the decorative backing board (see the photograph).

Fix the two frames together with masking tape, using the thicknesses of the frames as 'spacers' between the backing board and the organza, and the organza and the glass.

Have your work professionally framed in a box mount.

A Garden in My Heart
Robyn Rich

Robyn began embroidering thirteen years ago after developing some serious health problems, and found she really loved it. Robyn has always had a strong interest in the creative arts, particularly enjoying drawing and painting. She has also completed a Visual Merchandising Course at the Melbourne College of Decoration.

Robyn's embroidery business came about after she received an Achievement Award in a competition advertised in one of Australia's top embroidery magazines and made the front cover of the magazine. The phone didn't stop ringing and thus the mail order embroidery business, Robyn Rich Creations, specialising in hand-painted backgrounds, was born.

Initially Robyn designed a range of six embroidery kits with hand-painted backgrounds but as demand increased the range grew. The magazines also kept ringing and Robyn has now had over 30 pieces published in embroidery and craft magazines.

Robyn was thrilled to participate in *Embroidery from the Heart*. 'I knew straight away it was something I wanted to be involved in. Having health problems myself and spending quite a lot of time in hospital you get to see the wonderful job these Foundations do for research and to support people.'

When contemplating the theme for her piece, Robyn spoke to many nurses and people in hospital to find out what people go through with heart problems. 'It took me quite a while to come up with this piece; it needed to have meaning and I wanted it to be something that you see something new in every time you look at it … This is a heart full of life. I chose the cottage, because home is where the heart is; the path for the journey through life; the parterre garden for the crossroads in life; trees, flowers and gardens for renewing life, the lifeblood of our world; little quilts to represent friendship of the heart; and the virtues of Faith, Hope and Charity, representing the goodness in our hearts.'

Robyn may be contacted at: Robyn Rich Creations, PO Box 275, Crib Point Vic 3919, phone (03) 5983 9393
www.richcreations.com.au e-mail: robyn@richcreations.com.au

Stitches used: Back stitch, bullion stitch, detached chain stitch, fly stitch, French knot, lazy daisy stitch, running stitch, straight stitch.

MATERIALS REQUIRED

32 inch (80 cm) square seeded cream homespun
DMC stranded cotton:
  1 skein each: white, 422, 926, 928, 95, 3022,
  3023, 3042
  2 skeins each: 224, 225
  4 skeins: 523
Zig permanent pigment pen (brush #62 TC-4000), or
  brown double-ended marker, or fabric marker of
  your choice (must have fine tip)
Plaid folk art paints:
  Italian Sage Green 467
  Terracotta 433
  Coffee Bean 940
  Settler's Blue 607
  Rose Chiffon 753
Plaid textile medium (optional)
16 inch (40 cm) diameter embroidery hoop
paint brushes, sizes 2, 4, 6
needles:
  #8 straw
  #8 crewel

Please read the complete instructions before commencing.

Preparation for painting

Lay the design down on a firm surface and tape into place, then lay the piece of seeded homespun over the top and tape into place as well, centring the design and paying particular attention that the grain of the fabric is straight. The design should show through the fabric enough, but if you have trouble you can tape your work to a lightbox. Using the brush end of the Zig textile marker, mark in all of the lines on the design. Now carefully remove the design sheet from underneath. I suggest putting a blank piece of paper underneath and keeping the fabric taped down for painting.

Painting

The Plaid folk art paints can be used both full strength and diluted with water. If you want to wash your design you will need to add the textile medium. Make yourself up a palette of all five colours in different strengths—full strength, medium diluted, and very diluted in each colour.

You need to keep the brush as dry as possible when painting to prevent the colours from bleeding into each other. I suggest you practise on some scrap fabric until you get the desired effect.

Complete one little section at a time. Do not do all of the green areas over the whole design, for example, then all of the next colour, as you run the risk of smudging the paint. I also suggest ironing regularly to set the colour; press with a piece of cotton fabric over the top of your design with a warm iron.

Home is where the heart is

Terracotta Begin with the cottage roof, door and window boxes; using the size 4 brush apply soft strokes of medium diluted paint. Then again in soft strokes, using the same brush, paint the walls of the cottage and the path in very diluted paint.

Coffee Bean Using the size 4 brush, paint the tree trunks with soft strokes in a combination of medium and very diluted paint; make them darker on one side to create a shadow.

Sage Green Using the size 4 brush paint the foliage of the trees, these are painted using dabs of paint rather than strokes, in a combination of medium and very diluted paint, making them appear to be darker at the bottom. In full strength paint, using the size 2 brush, dab in the foliage in the window boxes and the garden.

Combination of sage green and terracotta In very diluted paint, using the size 6 brush, with soft strokes paint the background to give the effect of a soft wash; work one colour and then the other, do not mix them first.

Parterre garden

Sage Green Using the size 4 brush paint the garden sections in dabs of both full strength and medium diluted paint.

Scarecrow

Blue In very diluted paint, using the size 4 brush, apply soft strokes of very diluted paint to the

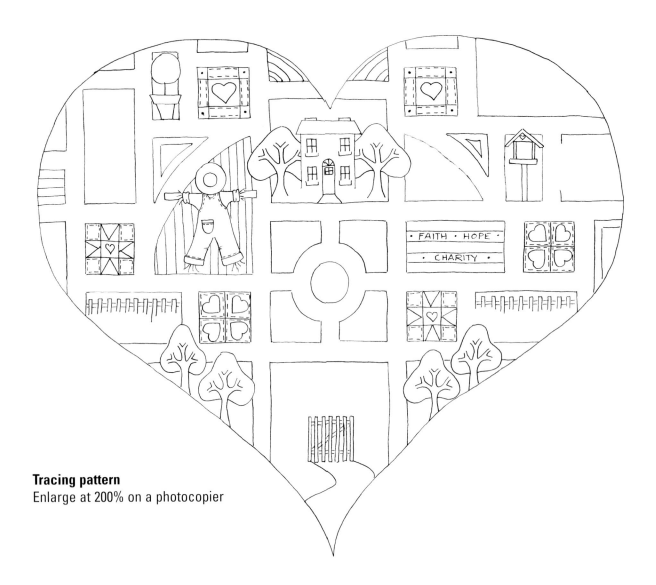

Tracing pattern
Enlarge at 200% on a photocopier

overalls, then in the areas there would naturally be shading apply some medium diluted paint.

Coffee Bean   Using the size 4 brush apply soft strokes of very diluted paint to the hat and the pole holding up the scarecrow, apply some medium diluted paint where there should be shadows.

Pink   Using the size 4 brush, apply soft strokes of very diluted paint to the shirt; again, you can apply some medium diluted paint to the areas that should be shaded—under the arms and where the shirt sleeves are rolled up.

Sage Green   Using the size 2 brush apply dabs of paint around the crown of the sunhat to appear like a circlet of flowers. Then using the size 6 brush apply soft strokes of very diluted paint to the background of this area.

Garden arch

Terracotta   Using the size 6 brush apply soft strokes of very diluted paint to the garden path, then in medium diluted paint using the size 4 brush add some shaded areas down the side of the path and under the gate. Using the size 2 brush apply soft strokes of very diluted paint to the upright pickets of the garden gate and to the support pieces behind. Then using medium diluted paint apply small soft strokes to the support pieces to add shading.

Sage Green Using the size 2 brush apply fine lines of full-strength paint to form the structure of the foxglove plants. Then using the size 4 brush apply dabs of full-strength paint to form the thick garden on the ground and the arch. Then in very diluted paint apply soft strokes to the area behind the foxgloves to create a wash.

Coffee Bean Using the size 6 brush apply soft strokes of very diluted paint to the background of this area.

Foxglove gardens

Sage Green Using the size 2 brush apply fine lines of full-strength paint to form the spikes of each foxglove, then apply strokes to form the leaves. Using the size 4 brush apply dabs of medium diluted paint to the areas between the plants, then in very diluted paint apply soft strokes of paint to the background of both areas.

Delphinium garden

Sage Green Using the size 2 brush apply fine lines of full-strength paint to form the spikes of each delphinium and then apply strokes to form the leaves. Using the size 4 brush apply dabs of medium strength paint to form the daisy bush in the background. Then in very diluted paint apply soft strokes to the background.

Terracotta Using the size 4 brush apply soft strokes to the upper area of the background above the sage green in very diluted paint.

Bird feeder

Terracotta Using the size 2 brush apply soft strokes of medium diluted paint to the post and the roof triangle of the bird feeder.

Sage Green Using the size 2 brush apply soft strokes of medium diluted paint to the rest of the bird feeder. Then using the size 4 brush and very diluted paint, apply soft strokes to the background of this area.

Rose bush

Sage Green Using the size 2 brush apply fine lines of full-strength paint to the stems of the rose bush. Then using the size 4 brush, apply dabs of medium diluted paint to form the foliage of the rose bush. Apply a combination of medium and very diluted paint to the lower area under the rose bush (refer to the photo).

Terracotta Using the size 4 brush apply soft strokes in very diluted paint to the area above the rose bush.

Six friendship quilts

For these you need to refer to the photo for placement of colours.

Sage Green Using the size 2 brush apply soft strokes of medium diluted paint to the green areas of each quilt.

Terracotta Using the size 2 brush apply soft strokes of very diluted paint to the terracotta areas of each quilt.

Lavender hedges

Terracotta Using the size 2 brush apply soft strokes of very diluted paint to the upright pickets of the fence. Then in medium diluted paint apply dabs of paint to the horizontal part of the fence; this creates shading, and makes it appear as though the horizontal piece is behind the uprights.

Sage Green Using the size 2 brush apply fine lines of full-strength paint to each spike of lavender. Then, using medium diluted paint, apply soft strokes of paint between the spikes of lavender and above and between the fence.

Virtues of Faith, Hope and Charity

Sage Green Using the size 2 brush apply soft strokes of very diluted paint to the areas where the rosebuds will be stitched.

Pink Using the size 2 brush apply soft strokes of very diluted paint to the areas where the virtues are written.

Six trees

Coffee Bean   Using the size 2 brush apply soft strokes of both medium and very diluted paint to the tree trunks, making one side darker than the other to create shading. Using the size 4 brush apply soft strokes of very diluted paint to the background of these areas.

Sage Green   Using the size 4 brush apply dabs of both full-strength and very diluted paint to the foliage areas of the trees, make them darker at the base, getting lighter at the top.

Topiary tree

Terracotta   Referring to the photo, use the size 2 brush and apply soft strokes of full-strength paint to the pot in the dark areas, then using a combination of medium and very diluted paint apply soft strokes to the pot.

Sage Green   Using the size 2 brush apply fine lines to form the bow, then apply dabs to the foliage of the topiary. Using the size 4 brush apply soft strokes of very diluted paint to the background.

Bud garden

Pink   Using the size 4 brush apply soft strokes of very diluted paint to two of the bud areas.

Sage green   Using the size 4 brush apply soft strokes of very diluted paint to the other two bud areas.

Hedges

Sage green   Using the size 4 brush apply dabs of full-strength paint to the hedges, and then apply soft dabs of medium paint to the areas between.

With a final press with a warm iron, the painting is now complete and you are ready to begin embroidering.

Embroidery

Tips

Thread length   Never work with a piece of thread longer than from your fingers to your elbow (approximately 18 inches or 45 cm), as it will twist, knot and become unmanageable.

Separating the threads   Take the colour you are to use, cut to length as above, and separate the six strands. Then, depending on the number of strands you are to use, place them back together and they are ready to use. This will prevent the thread from twisting.

Embroidery hoop   It is a good idea to use an embroidery hoop as it keeps your work taut and you will end up with a neater piece of work.

Needles   The #8 straw needle is used for all bullion stitches and French knots. The #8 crewel needle is used for all of the other stitches.

Outer border

Thread the crewel needle with 3 strands of DMC 523 and work a band of very close French knots, 2 wraps each. Make them very close to give a hedge-like appearance.

Home is where the heart is

Window boxes   Thread the straw needle with 1 strand of DMC 225 and scatter 2-wrap French knots in the window boxes. Repeat with single strands of DMC 224 and DMC 523.

The garden   This is worked in 2 strands of DMC thread a variety of colours—white, 224, 225, 523, 928, 3023, 3042. You can refer to the photo or place the colours where you choose. The flowers are worked in French knots using the straw needle; vary the number of wraps to create texture, as in a real garden, flowers vary in size.

Parterre garden

Thread the straw needle with 2 strands of DMC 523 and work the outer lines of the garden. The flowers are worked in French knots in a variety of colours—DMC 224, 225, 523, 928, 950, 3023, 3042—using the straw needle and 2 strands. Again vary the number of wraps to create texture. You can refer to the photo or choose your own placement; the only thing I do suggest is that you stitch the knots in clumps of colour to appear like bushes.

Scarecrow

Sunhat Thread the straw needle with 2 strands of DMC 950 and work single-wrap French knots around the crown, then thread the needle with 2 strands of DMC 523 and work more single-wrap French knots between the knots in the first colour.

Overalls Thread the crewel needle with 1 strand of DMC 926 and work the stitching on the overalls in running stitch.

Straw Thread the crewel needle with 2 strands of DMC 422 and work a series of short straight stitches to give the appearance of straw poking out from the cuffs and trouser legs.

Daisies Thread the crewel needle with 2 strands of white and work 5-petalled daisies in lazy daisy stitch. Then thread the straw needle with 2 strands of DMC 422 and work a single French knot in the centre of each daisy. The stems are worked in a single straight stitch using 2 strands of DMC 523 in the crewel needle. You will need to use a couple of anchoring stitches for the curved stems, placing them where the leaves will begin. Work the leaves in detached chain stitch; referring to the photo for placement.

Foliage Between the daisies are 3-wrap French knot leaves worked in 2 strands of DMC 523 using the straw needle.

Garden arch

Foxgloves Thread the straw needle with 2 strands of DMC 225 and work each of the light pink foxgloves in a series of French knots. See photo for placement. Begin at the top of the spire with 1 single-wrap French knot, work another two the

same, then work two single-wrap French knots side by side. Work your way down the flower spike, stitching pairs of French knots, and increasing the number of wraps as you go down the flower spike, following the diagram. Thread the straw needle with 2 strands of DMC 224 and repeat this process for the darker pink foxgloves. The foxglove stems and leaves are worked in 2 strands of DMC 523; the stems in a single straight stitch and the leaves in detached chain stitch.

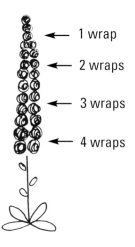

The garden Thread the straw needle with 2 strands of DMC 928 and work small delphinium plants in a series of 2-wrap French knots, starting with a single knot at the top and working pairs of French knots below. See photo for placement. Work the stems and leaves in 2 strands of DMC 3022, the stems in straight stitch and the leaves in detached chain stitch. Then using the straw needle work clumps of French knots, 2 strands in each of DMC 224, 225 and 3042, then place DMC 523 and 3023 between them to form leaves. Make the garden very thick with lots of flowers.

The arch Thread the straw needle with 2 strands of DMC 225 and work 2-wrap French knots scattered over the arch. Thread the same needle with 2 strands of DMC 3023 and work 2-wrap French knot leaves in among the roses.

Foxglove gardens

Foxgloves Thread the straw needle with 2 strands of DMC 225; work all of the light pink foxgloves in a series of French knots, following the above instructions. Then thread the straw needle with 2 strands of DMC 224 and work all of the darker pink foxgloves. The stems and leaves are worked in 2 strands of DMC 523 using the crewel needle. The stems are each worked in a single straight stitch and the leaves in a series of detached chain stitch.

Foliage   Between the foxgloves are a series of 2-wrap French knots in DMC 523 worked with the straw needle.

Delphinium garden

Delphiniums   Thread the straw needle with 2 strands of DMC 928 and work the light blue delphiniums in a series of French knots. Follow the instructions for the foxgloves. Repeat this for the darker blue delphiniums in DMC 926. The stems and leaves are worked using the crewel needle in 2 strands of DMC 3023; the stems in a single straight stitch and the leaves in a series of detached chain stitches.

Daisy bush   Thread the crewel needle with 2 strands of DMC 224 and work daisies scattered across the bush in lazy daisy stitch. Then thread the straw needle with 2 strands of white and work a single-wrap French knot in the centre of each daisy. Thread the crewel needle with 2 strands of DMC 3023 and work leaves in detached chain stitch between the daisies. If the bush needs to appear thicker, work some French knots in the same thread, using the straw needle. The stem should be worked in straight stitch in 2 strands of DMC 3023.

Foliage   Thread the straw needle with 2 strands of DMC 523 and work a series of 2-wrap French knots in between the plants.

Bird feeder

The bird   Thread the straw needle with 1 strand of DMC 3022 and work 3 vertical bullion stitches, each using 6 wraps, to form the body. Then work 2 horizontal bullion stitches to form the head, again using 6 wraps. Then work a series of tiny straight stitches out at an angle from the base of the bird for the wings. Thread the straw needle with 1 strand of

DMC 422 and work a 2-wrap French knot in the centre of the head for the beak.

Daisies   Thread the crewel needle with 2 strands of white and work the daisies in lazy daisy stitch. Thread the crewel needle with 2 strands of DMC 422 and work a single-wrap French knot in the centre of each daisy. The stems and leaves are worked in 2 strands of DMC 523 using the crewel needle; the stems are worked in straight stitch using an anchoring stitch to curve them, placing the anchoring stitch where the leaves will begin. Work the leaves in detached chain stitch.

Foliage   Thread the straw needle with 2 strands of DMC 523, and work 2-wrap French knot in among the daisies.

Rose bush

Thread the straw needle with 2 strands of DMC 224 and for each rose centre or bud centre work 2 bullion stitches side by side, using 6 wraps. Thread the straw needle with 2 strands of DMC 225 and work 3 bullions wrapped around the rose centres to form the roses, each stitch using 15 wraps. Then work bullion stitches either side of the bud centres, using 8 wraps, to form the buds. To make the tiny buds, thread the straw needle with 2 strands of DMC 224 and scatter 2-wrap French knots over the bush. Thread the crewel needle with 2 strands of DMC 523 and work the stems in straight stitch. Thread the straw needle with 2 strands of the same colour and work French knots massed in among the roses, varying the number of wraps to create texture.

Six friendship quilts

Thread the crewel needle with 1 strand of DMC 3023, and on each quilt work running stitches to give the appearance of hand-stitching on a quilt.

Lavender hedges

Thread the crewel needle with 2 strands of DMC 3042 and work each lavender spike in a series of detached chain stitches. Thread the crewel needle with 2 strands of DMC 3023 and work the stem of each spike in a straight stitch.

Virtues

Wording Thread the crewel needle with 1 strand of DMC 3023 and work the lettering in tiny back stitches, then work the dots in single-wrap French knots.

Buds Thread the straw needle with 2 strands of DMC 224 and work each bud in a pair of horizontal bullion stitches, each one using 6 wraps. Thread the crewel needle with 2 strands of DMC 523 and work a fly stitch with a double calyx and a longer anchoring stitch from the stem. Then work the leaves in detached chain stitch in the same thread.

Topiary tree

Thread the straw needle with 2 strands of DMC 224 and work 2-wrap French knot roses. Thread the same needle with 2 strands of DMC 523 and work 2-wrap French knot leaves between the roses.

Bud garden

Thread the straw needle with 2 strands of DMC 224 and work the buds, each of 2 horizontal bullion stitches, 6 wraps each. Thread the crewel needle with 2 strands of DMC 523 and work the calyxes with fly stitch with a double calyx and a longer anchoring stitch to form the stem. Then work the leaves in detached chain stitch.

Hedges

Green hedges Thread the straw needle with 2 strands of DMC 523 and work rows of 3-wrap French knots. Refer to the photo for the number of rows.

Inner gardens Referring to the photo for colour placement, work the inner garden in 2 strands of DMC 224, 225, 823, 928 and 3032 in French knots, varying the number of wraps to create texture.

Finished

Your wonderful piece is now completed and can be professionally framed to hang in your house so you can spend many happy hours gazing at it. I hope you enjoy painting and stitching this as much as I did. Happy stitching!

'And Time Remembered is Grief Forgotten'

(*Atalanta in Calydon* by Algernon Charles Swinburne 1837 – 1909)

Carolyn Anne Pearce

Carolyn was taught to stitch by her mother and has always been fascinated by textiles, lace and ribbons. As a child she spent her pocket money on special bits and pieces of treasures and as she grew older would pore over the needlework patterns in her mother's English *Women's Journal*.

Carolyn 'paints with her threads, bringing the pictures in her mind to life'. She does a rough sketch on paper, gathers together threads and ribbons and places them together where she can keep glancing at them as she works around the house.

She finds inspiration from many beautiful things in nature such as the movement of the leaves and branches in the wind and the darting of the birds around her garden. Her home is filled with flowers and beautiful objects including paintings of flowers, books and china.

Carolyn writes for an embroidery magazine and is very busy teaching embroidery in Sydney as well as country areas and interstate. She believes that teaching needlework is far more than just passing on knowledge- it is the sharing of ideas, helping and learning constantly from each other. 'Having to explain to others what I do and why has helped me to a better understanding of what I tend to do by instinct.' She loves to sit and immerse herself in her stitching, losing herself in a glorious world of threads and ribbons.

Carolyn agreed to participate in *Embroidery from the Heart* believing 'there is no better purpose in life than to give pleasure and help to others. I have been given so much help by students and suppliers over the years… this is a wonderful chance to give something back.' She also believes that needlework can be a solace when all around us is chaos.

Carolyn uses a variety of weights and textures of thread to give a sense of depth and changing light to her embroidery. For this project she has created a large silk ribboned heart using four different threads and one silk ribbon for the leaves The use of the heavy, shiny Ophir thread, paired with a fine dull silk which recedes in the background, and combined with the fine metallic thread for the leaves on the sprays of rosebuds, creates a wonderful play of light and gives a dainty appearance to the overall work.

Carolyn may be contacted through: The Crewel Gobelin, 9 Marion Street, Killara NSW 2071, phone (02) 9498 6831 www.thecrewelgobelin.com.au   e-mail: crewelgobelin@bigpond.com.au

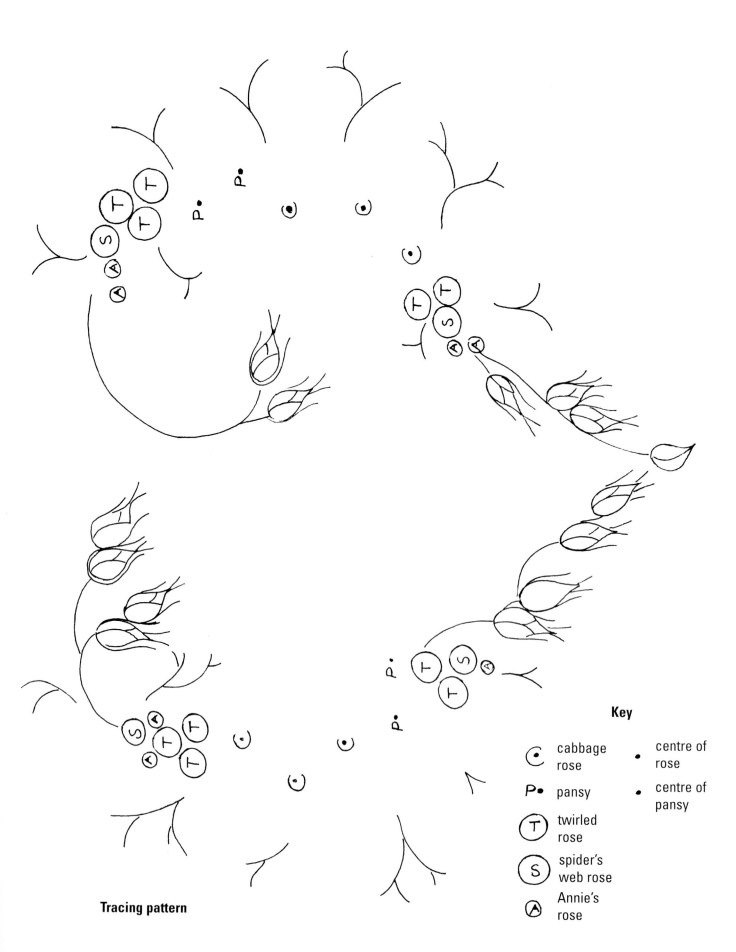

Tracing pattern

Key

- **C·** cabbage rose
- **P·** pansy
- **T** twirled rose
- **S** spider's web rose
- **A** Annie's rose
- **·** centre of rose
- **·** centre of pansy

Note: Where the threads or silk ribbons specified are not readily available you can substitute, using the photograph as a colour guide.

Stitches used: Annie's rose, back stitch, cabbage rose, colonial knot, fly stitch, French knot, ruched pansies, smocker's knot, spider's web rose, stem stitch, straight stitch, twirled rose.

MATERIALS REQUIRED

20 x 40 inches (50 x 100 cm) cream furnishing fabric
   or moiré taffeta
20 inch (50 cm) square pelon (interlining)
13 mm silk ribbons:
   Kacoonda #310, 24 inches (60 cm)
   Kacoonda #101, 24 inches (60 cm)
   Kacoonda 6C, 1 ¼ yd (1 m)
   YLI #163, 12 inches (30 cm)
7 mm silk ribbons:
   YLI #159, 20 inches (50 cm)
   YLI #178, 8 inches (20 cm)
   Colour Streams Rose Blush, 1 ¾ yd (1.5 m)
   Colour Streams Specially Dyed for Pansies,
   8 inches (20 cm)
   Vintage Ribbons Moonlight, 6 inches (15 cm)
   Vintage Ribbons Old Gold, 6 inches (15 cm)
   Vintage Ribbons Vintage Rose, 1 ¼ yd (1 m)
4 mm silk ribbons:
   Vintage Ribbons Antique Rose, 2 ¼ yd (2 m)
   Colourstreams Rose Blush, 3 ⅓ yd (3 m)
   Glen Lorin Green Sands, 2 ¼ yd (2 m)
   YLI #76, 12 inches (30 cm)
   Thread Gatherer's Silken Ribbons, Heirloom Blue
   Toray Sillook #726, 1 ¼ yd (1 m)
threads:
   DMC stranded cotton #640
   Caron Waterlilies, Orange Blossom
   Colourstreams Ophir twisted silk, Tuscan Olive
   Kacoonda fine silk #104 and #106
   Kacoonda 2-ply silk #305
   YLI silk floss #181
   Reflections metallic yarn #403
   Rajmahal #311
machine threads:
   to match ribbons (a neutral colour works well)
needles:
   chenille #18, #22
   crewel #5, # 8, #10
   straw #10
   sharps #12

10 inch (25 cm) embroidery hoop with adjustable
   tightening screw, inner ring bound with cotton
   tape
2B pencil
light box

Preparation

Cut the cream furnishing fabric into two 20 inch (50 cm) squares, putting one aside for use in framing. If you are using moiré taffeta, adjust at this point so that the design will be centred on the stripes. Lay your fabric over the design, matching centres, and pin securely.

Using the light box and a very sharp 2B pencil, trace the stems for the spray of rosebuds and the fine stems for the spray of pink knot flowers. Mark the centres of the cabbage roses and the ruched pansies with a dot.

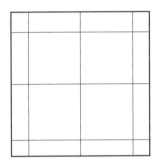

Diagram 1

Pin the pelon to the wrong side of the fabric and baste in a grid (diagram 1). Zigzag the raw edges to prevent fraying.

Order of work: Cabbage roses, ruched pansies, twirled roses, spider's web roses, Annie's roses, rosebuds, silk ribbon leaves, stems, fly-stitch leaves, pink knot sprays, blue loop flowers, tiny forget-me-nots.

Use the embroidery hoop for all silk ribbon work and the sprays of pale pink knot flowers.

Cabbage roses

Start by making the individual petals for each of the 6 cabbage roses. Each petal is just over 1 inch (25 mm) in length. I quite ruthlessly cut the ribbon to take advantage of the shading; it is a good idea to make more petals than you actually need so that you can try different combinations. (Tip: use a plastic floss box with compartments in which to keep each set of petals.)

For each rose, using 13 mm ribbons:

Kacoonda 310 (deepest tone), cut 3 petals

Kacoonda 101, cut 4 or 5 petals (number depends on how tightly they are gathered)

Kacoonda 6C (palest tone), cut 5 or 6 petals (number depends on how tightly they are gathered)

YLI #163, cut 2 petals

Diagram 2: Making a petal

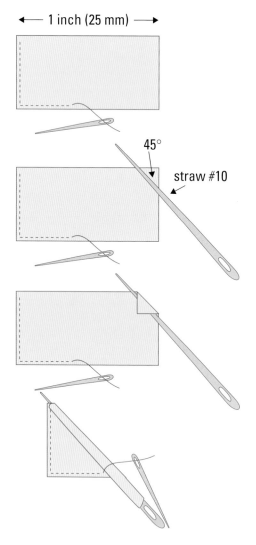

← 1 inch (25 mm) →

45°

straw #10

Tip: have a small piece of wet sponge in a dish next to you to moisten your finger tips—this makes rolling the ribbon easier.

Thread matching fine machine thread in a sharp #12 and stitch as illustrated in diagram 2. Start with a knot and a back stitch. Take tiny stitches as close to the edge of the ribbon as possible.

Pin the straw #10 into the top right hand corner of the ribbon.

Fold the top right-hand corner of the ribbon downwards over the straw needle. Moisten your fingertips and roll the ribbon around the needle so that it lines up with the knot at the start.

Pick up the dangling needle and thread and take a stitch through the roll, remove the straw needle and pull up the gathering thread so that the petal cups slightly. Secure with two back stitches. Cut off the thread.

Experiment with various petals, stopping at different points when rolling the upper right-hand corner. You will achieve a more open look to a petal if you stop a little way from the securing knot.

I arrange the petals as though you were looking down on the rose. There are three rows of petals in each rose, with three petals of the deepest tone in the first row, 4 or 5 middle tone petals in the second and 5 or 6 of the palest petals in the outer row. For the first two rows, the roll of the petals faces outwards. For the outermost row, the roll of the petal faces toward the centre of the rose.

To construct the rose

Make the central colonial knot in 7 mm YLI #159. Stitch the tails of the knot flat on the back of your work, then with the same thread take a tiny invisible stab stitch up through the knot. Bring your needle to the front of your work, just next to the knot, ready to attach the first petal. I use the minimum number of stitches to attach the petals until the rose is complete. This makes it easier to unpick and rearrange the petals if you are not happy with a particular rose. Tidy the petals before attaching them, by trimming away any whiskers of thread or ribbon. Snip off the stump of the ribbon roll on the right-hand side of the petals as close to the fastening-off knot as possible (diagram 3).

Diagram 3

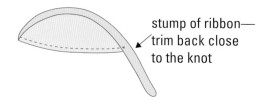

stump of ribbon—
trim back close
to the knot

For the first two layers of petals the roll is facing outward. Attach each petal by stabbing from the front to the back of the petal at the left-hand end of the roll, just above the beginning of the line of gathering stitches. Take the needle to the back of your work, next to where the thread is emerging. Slightly cup the petals and re-emerge at the right-hand end of the petal position, stab the petal from front to back and return to the back of your work as before, re-emerging one-third to halfway along the base of the first petal. Attach the second petal in the same manner. Repeat for the third petal, this time coming up one-third to halfway along the lower edge of the second petal. The third petal will overlap the first petal on the outside. Whether the petals overlap by one-third or one-half depends on how tightly you pull them up when you make them, and also on how big the centre knot is.

Diagram 4

petals 1, 2, 3:
13 mm Kacoonda 310
centre colonial knot:
7 mm YLI #159

The second row of four petals also faces outward. You could use three petals of Kacoonda 101 and one petal of YLI #163, or two petals of each. The petals of the final row face toward the centre of the rose. The last petal for the row returns to the inside of the circle (diagram 5).

Diagram 5

When you are happy with your arrangement, use the eye of a large chenille needle to push any tails of the thread in underneath the petals and then stab-stitch to secure.

Ruched pansies

There are four ruched pansies, two on each side of the heart design, one in each colour combination.

For the petals, cut 4 x 1 ⅜ inch (28 mm) lengths each of Vintage Moonlight and Vintage Old Gold, and 2 x 3 ⅜ inch (84 mm) lengths each of Colour Streams specially dyed ribbon for pansies and YLI #178.

Overlap two 1 ⅜ inch (28 mm) pieces of ribbon for the back petals as illustrated in diagram 6B, pinning diagonally. Stitch as shown, using a sharp #12. Make two sets in Moonlight and two in Old Gold.

Draw in the row of stitches (not too tightly) so that the petals form a slight arc with a pointed tail in the centre, as shown in diagram 6B. Back-stitch to secure the thread.

Diagram 6A

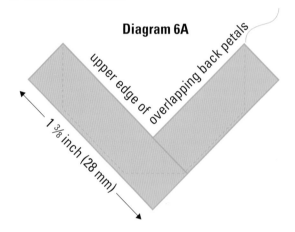

Diagram 6B

For the lower petals, fold an 84 mm length of ribbon into thirds as shown in diagram 7, using pins if necessary to hold the diagonals.

Stitch as shown. Big stitches will gather smaller. Draw in the gathers tightly and back-stitch to secure. Don't cut off the thread. Take your needle through the starting knot to form a circle. Back-stitch. The two side petals will meet in a sweet heart shape and there should be just a tiny hole in the centre.

Diagram 7

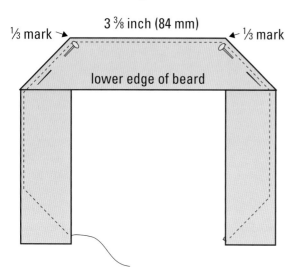

3 ⅜ inch (84 mm)

⅓ mark

⅓ mark

lower edge of beard

up from the fabric. Now take about 6–8 running stitches down the middle of the ribbon, using a stitch length of about ¼ inch (5 mm). Push the needle partway through the fabric, close to where the ribbon is emerging (make sure the last stitch is the same size as the rest or you can end up with a rather large petal). Tighten the knot on the needle, then pull the needle all the way through to the back. The ribbon folds up into petals with a knot in the middle—so sweet, so easy! You can adjust the petals with the eye of a needle so that they lie in different directions. Make seven of these roses.

Rosebuds

Using a chenille #22, begin with a detached twisted chain stitch for the centre petal. For the ribbon-stitch side petals come out slightly to one side at the base of the bud, and cross over to the opposite side at least two-thirds up the side of the centre petal. Repeat for the second petal on opposite side of the bud. Then repeat for sepals. The rosebud is softened with straight stitches and a fly stitch in 1 strand of DMC 640, using crewel #10.

Attach the back petals behind the lower petals securely, so that they sit up well above the lower petals.

Attach the pansies to the background fabric with invisible stab stitches around the centre hole, then work a colonial knot in the hole with 4 mm YLI #76 using a chenille #22 needle.

Twirled roses and spider's web rose

There are ten twirled roses and four spider's web roses. Refer to the diagram for placement. (**Tip**: start each flower next to the flower you have just finished to minimise problems of spacing.)

The twirled roses are worked in 7 mm ribbons—Colourstreams Rose Blush and Vintage Ribbons Vintage Rose. The spider's web roses are worked in 4 mm ribbons—Vintage Ribbons Antique Rose and Colourstreams Rose Blush. Work the 7 mm ribbon with the chenille #18 and the 4 mm ribbon with the chenille #22, using machine threads to match for.

Annie's rose

Thread the 4 mm Rose Blush ribbon into a chenille #22. Bring to the right side of your work. Wrap the ribbon around the needle as though doing a colonial knot, but at least 2–2 ¼ inches (5–6 cm)

Diagram 8

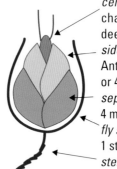

centre petal, detached twisted chain stitch: 4 mm Antique Rose, deepest colour

side petals, ribbon stitch: 4 mm Antique Rose, palest colour, or 4 mm Rose Blush

sepals, ribbon stitch: 4 mm Green Sands

fly stitch and straight stitches: 1 strand DMC 640

stem stitch: 1 strand DMC 640

Silk ribbon leaves

Using a chenille #22 and the 4 mm Green Sands silk ribbon, work a few ribbon-stitch leaves and a few twisted detached chain leaves in among the silk ribbon flowers. The twisted detached chain leaves are highlighted with a straight stitch at the tip of each leaf and a smocker's knot (see stitch glossary) at the base of the leaf, worked with 1 strand Kacoonda 104 fine silk.

Finishing touches

The fly-stitch leaves, the spray of pink knot flowers, the blue loop-stitch flowers and the tiny blue forget-me-nots are worked as finishing touches, using the photograph as a guide.

Stems

All stems are worked in stem stitch in 1 strand of DMC 640, using the crewel #10.

Fly-stitch leaves

Next to the cabbage roses, work a pair of fly-stitch leaves; for the lower leaf use 1 strand of Ophir twisted silk, Tuscan Olive, in the crewel #5; for the upper leaf use 1 strand of Kacoonda 106 in the #8 crewel.

The smaller fly-stitch leaves on the sprays of rosebuds are worked in alternating pairs of 1 strand of Kacoonda 104 (#8 crewel) and 1 strand of YLI metallic yarn 403 (straw #10). Once the silk leaves are embroidered, work random straight stitches in the metallic thread between the silk fly stitches.

All fly-stitch leaves are finished with a smocker's knot.

Sprays of pink knot flowers

Embroider these flowers with the work in the hoop. Work tiny back stitches (it is easiest to stab each stitch) for the stems in 1 strand of Rajmahal 311 using the crewel #10. Work the flowers in 2 strands of Caron Waterlilies Orange Blossom, using the crewel #8, mainly in colonial knots. Add some 1-wrap French knots in the same thread at the tips and along the edges of the sprays.

Blue loop-stitch flowers

Using the 4 mm Toray Sillook #726 ribbon in the chenille #22, work a tight colonial knot for the centre of each flower; secure the tails at the back of the work with machine thread, leaving the thread dangling. For the petals, use the 4 mm Thread Gatherer's Heirloom Blue ribbon in the chenille #22, making five loop-stitch petals (the diameter of a chenille #13 needle) worked very close to the centre knot. Secure each petal at the back of the work with machine thread in a sharps #12. Gently pull each petal to make sure it is secure.

Tiny blue forget-me-nots

Using 3 strands of YLI silk floss #181 in the crewel #8, work a colonial knot for the centre of each flower. In 1 strand of Kacoonda 2-ply silk #305, work five colonial knots for the petals.

Completion

Remove all basting threads, and press the work carefully, face down on a thick towel, if necessary. Another 20 inch (50 cm) square of the fabric used for the embroidery can be used to cover a mount, as suggested by Art Scene in Ryde, Sydney, for the framing of my embroidered piece.

Heart Flutter
Catherine Howell

Catherine comes from a family of artists—her grandmother was an artist, her father a carpenter and her mother a floral designer. Born in England, she spent her childhood in the picturesque Cotswolds and also spent time in Lusaka, Zambia where she was encouraged by her teachers to pursue needlework. She later attended the Gloucestershire College of Art and Design in Cheltenham, England, majoring in fashion and textiles.

Catherine moved to Australia 21 years ago after meeting her husband. She currently lives with her family in an old property with a large garden in Mount Eliza on the Mornington Peninsula in Victoria.

Catherine is well known for her style of dimensional embroidery and her passion for replicating nature in her work. She loves to experiment with combinations of silk ribbon, threads and hand-dyed wools in rich colours to create three-dimensional pictures of flowers and leaves, inspired by her extensive garden and childhood memories of English gardens and hedgerows. She also spends a lot of time walking and exploring the bushland near her home. One of her earliest pieces of faux stumpwork embroidery was inspired by an armful of colourful autumn leaves collected during a walk.

Catherine was delighted to be asked to create a piece of work around the heart. Having survived a life-threatening illness herself, she felt this would be a wonderful way of giving something back to the world and bringing joy to others.

Catherine's rich, three-dimensional flowered heart, in warm colours of ruby and pink, bursting open to reveal a surge of butterflies, was inspired by her research into the happy, healthy heart.

Catherine teaches her approach to dimensional embroidery locally and throughout Australia. She finds great satisfaction and happiness in encouraging her students to be creative and experiment with different colours and textures in their embroidery.

Catherine may be contacted at: Overport Lodge, 148 Overport Road, South Frankston Vic 3119,
phone/fax (03) 9787 9425
e-mail: clhowelldesign@aol.com

Template A: Main heart pattern
(cut 1)
enlarge to 166% on a photocopier

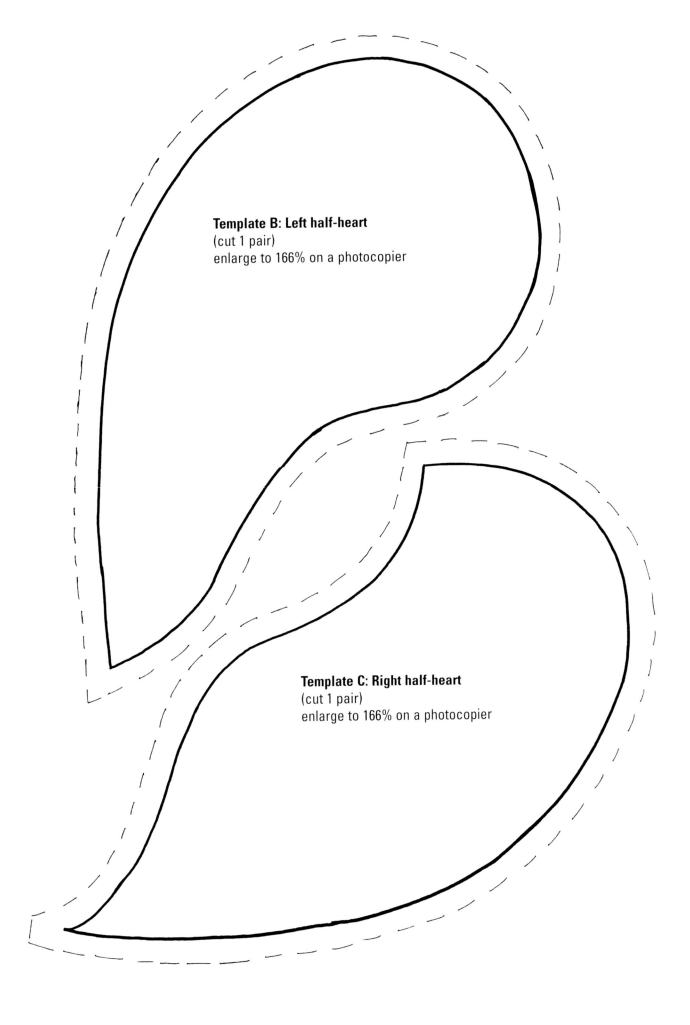

Template B: Left half-heart
(cut 1 pair)
enlarge to 166% on a photocopier

Template C: Right half-heart
(cut 1 pair)
enlarge to 166% on a photocopier

'Heart Flutter' combines the different textures of wool, silk thread and silk ribbons in a large piece mounted in a deep box frame.

Stitches used: Back stitch, blanket stitch, bullion stitch, drizzle stitch, French knot, lazy daisy stitch, long and short satin stitch, pistil stitch, ribbon stitch, satin stitch, slip stitch, stem stitch, straight stitch, Turkey stitch.

Note: Where the brands of thread or ribbon specified are not readily available, you can substitute using the photograph as a colour guide.

MATERIALS REQUIRED

22 x 20 in (55 x 50 cm) deep rose hand-dyed linen
16 in (40 cm) square deep ruby sateen fabric
14 x 32 in (36 x 80 cm) deep rose hand-dyed wool
    flannel
1 ¼ in (35 mm) hand-painted silk ribbon in white and
    rose, 1 ⅔ yd (1.5 m)
10 x 12 in (25 x 30 cm) deep ruby organza
Kacoonda fine wools: natural, #9A, 17, 85, 104, 108
Kacoonda mohair: #9A, 108
Kacoonda fine silk: #8E
Kacoonda thick silk: #3C
Kacoonda 2-ply silk: #107
Kacoonda silk ribbon #104:
    7 mm x 20 inches (50 cm)
    4 mm x 1 ¼ yd (1 m)
Gumnut Yarns Daisies: #050, 624, 626, 628, 629,
    850, 991
Gumnut Yarns Buds #647
Rajmahal art silk: #65, 96, 379
Appleton crewel wool #948
Anchor Marlitt #1076
DMC Broderie Medici wool #8110
Kreinik Metallics Blending Filament #093
12 inch (30 cm) squares of felt: one each in white, mid
    pink, crimson and mid green
mid pink and dark ruby machine thread for stitching
needles:
    #7, #8 crewel
    #5 milliner's
water-erasable pen
polyester wadding (about 4 handfuls)

Preparation

Tack a line down the centre and across the middle of the deep rose hand-dyed linen in contrasting thread. (This will be removed when you have completed the embroidery.)

Cut out the main heart piece in the ruby sateen fabric, using template A. Machine along the stitch line, clip the ½ inch (1 cm) seam allowance with scissors and position on the background fabric. Pin into place, truing the edge under, then stitch into place with tiny slip-stitches, leaving an opening along the lower right-hand side large enough to insert the wadding. When you have padded out the shape sufficiently to give the heart a rounded look—to a maximum of about 1 inch (3 cm) in the middle), close the opening with small slip-stitches.

Mark the outlines of the two half-heart pieces (templates B and C) onto the rose hand-dyed wool flannel. Leave sufficient fabric around them for turning the edges under and to set each in an embroidery hoop if desired. Cut two backing pieces to match.

Mark the positions of the essential elements of the stumpwork and the flat embroidery design from the design chart using the water-erasable pen. Note that the shaded areas and the forget-me-nots are stitched directly onto the flannel.

Embroidery

Use the crewel needles for the ribbon and wool work and the milliner's needle for the finer embroidery.

Clematis

Mark out 12 clematis petals on the white felt following the flower and leaf template, using the water-erasable pen. Start by stitching the outside of the petals in blanket stitch with Gumnut Daisies 050. Follow diagram 1 for the positioning of the colours and stitching direction (note the slant of the stitches). The middle is stitched with long and short satin stitch in Kacoonda mohair 108. Blend between the two colours with straight stitch in Kacoonda mohair 9A. Overlay two straight stitches in the middle of the petal with a single strand of Rajmahal 96.

Cut out the petals, then arrange two flowers of six petals in position on the right half-heart. Stitch into place, allowing a gap in the centre of each flower about ½ inch (1 cm) in diameter. Fill the centre with Turkey stitch in Kacoonda fine wool 17 and 85 (1 strand of each colour in the same

Flower and leaf templates

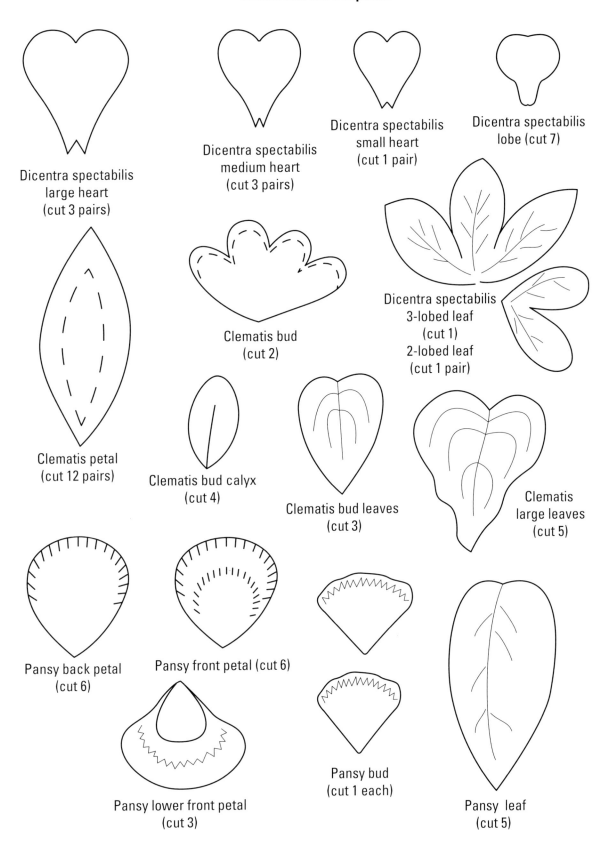

Dicentra spectabilis
large heart
(cut 3 pairs)

Dicentra spectabilis
medium heart
(cut 3 pairs)

Dicentra spectabilis
small heart
(cut 1 pair)

Dicentra spectabilis
lobe (cut 7)

Clematis bud
(cut 2)

Dicentra spectabilis
3-lobed leaf
(cut 1)
2-lobed leaf
(cut 1 pair)

Clematis petal
(cut 12 pairs)

Clematis bud calyx
(cut 4)

Clematis bud leaves
(cut 3)

Clematis
large leaves
(cut 5)

Pansy back petal
(cut 6)

Pansy front petal (cut 6)

Pansy bud
(cut 1 each)

Pansy lower front petal
(cut 3)

Pansy leaf
(cut 5)

needle). Trim to a neat mounded shape, then work 10 x 30-wrap drizzle stitches in the very centre of the mound in Anchor Marlitt 1076 and Gumnut Buds 647 (1 strand of each in the same needle). Scatter approximately 6 drizzle stitches around the Turkey stitches, and place 4 in the centre, using DMC Broderie Medici 8110 (single strand, 30 wraps).

Diagram 1 Clematis petal

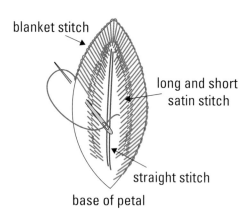

blanket stitch

long and short satin stitch

straight stitch

base of petal

Diagram 2 Clematis leaf

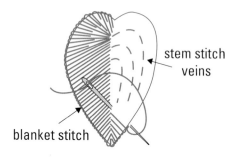

stem stitch veins

blanket stitch

Mark the 5 large and 3 smaller clematis leaves onto the green felt. Buttonhole the leaves in Kacoonda fine wool 104 (see diagram 2, then stem-stitch the veins of the larger leaves in 2 strands of Gumnut Buds 647. Work the mid-veins on the smaller leaves in Gumnut Buds 647 and the side veins in Kacoonda fine silk 8E. Cut out the leaves and stitch into position around the clematis flowers, adding the stems in stem stitch in Kacoonda fine wool 104.

Blanket-stitch the 2 buds from the template sheet on crimson felt in Kacoonda fine wool 108;

edge-stitch one of the buds with blanket stitch in Gumnut Daisies 050. Stitch the four 'petals' for the calyces in blanket stitch on green felt with Gumnut daisies 624. Cut out the petals and bud leaves, assemble as in diagram 3, and stitch into place at the top of the right half-heart.

Diagram 3 Clematis bud assembly

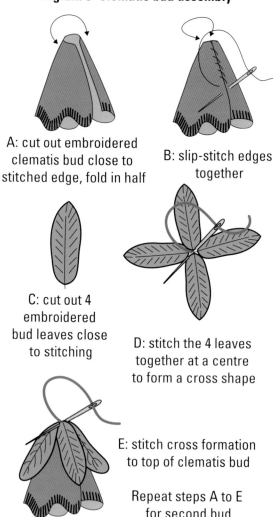

A: cut out embroidered clematis bud close to stitched edge, fold in half

B: slip-stitch edges together

C: cut out 4 embroidered bud leaves close to stitching

D: stitch the 4 leaves together at a centre to form a cross shape

E: stitch cross formation to top of clematis bud

Repeat steps A to E for second bud

Dicentra spectabilis (Bleeding heart or Dutchman's trousers)

Trace 3 large pairs, 3 medium pairs and 1 small pair of flower shapes from the template sheet onto the crimson felt. Fill these shapes with blanket stitch (see diagram 4) in Gumnut Daisies 850.

Then blanket-stitch 7 single lobe shapes (from the template sheet) onto white felt in Gumnut Daisies 990. Cut out all the shapes, close to the outside of the blanket stitches, then stitch the heart-shaped flowers together in pairs, inserting a small amount of wadding before closing (see diagram 4). Insert one lobe shape at a 45-degree angle at the base of each heart. Work a 15-wrap bullion stitch in Gumnut Daisies 850 on each side of the lobes. Stitch the stems in stem stitch with 2 strands of Rajmahal 379.

Work two smaller flowers directly on the background (shaded shapes), using the same threads.

Blanket-stitch the leaf shapes onto the green felt with Gumnut Daisies 628, working the veins in stem stitch in Kacoonda 2-ply silk 107. Cut out and stitch the 3-lobed leaf onto the background, following the flower placement diagram, then embroider the two 2-lobed leaves in long and short satin stitch in Gumnut Daisies 628.

Pansies

Mark all the pansy petals onto the mid-pink felt. Blanket stitch the six back petals in Appleton crewel wool 948, and edge them in an open blanket stitch in Kacoonda natural fine wool.

Blanket-stitch the edges of the six front petals in Kacoonda fine wool 108 (see diagram 5). Fill the middles in satin stitch in DMC Broderie Medici 8110. Edge these petals in open blanket stitch and scatter a few straight stitches between the two colours in Kacoonda natural fine wool. Overlay a few straight stitches in a single strand of Rajmahal 379.

Diagram 4 Dicentra flower

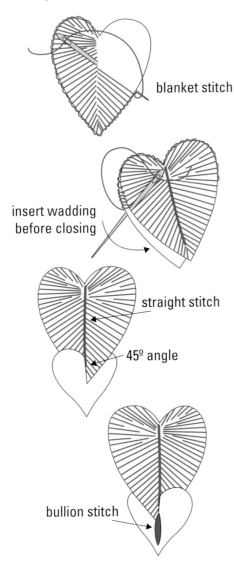

blanket stitch

insert wadding before closing

straight stitch

45º angle

bullion stitch

Diagram 5 Pansy

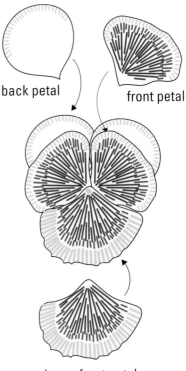

back petal

front petal

lower front petal

Flower placement
Shaded areas indicate
embroidery worked directly
onto the background.

Work the edges of the three lower front petals in dense blanket stitch in Kacoonda natural fine wool. Next, work long and short satin stitch in Kacoonda fine wool 108. The centre is satin-stitched in DMC Broderie Medici 8110. Overlay a few straight stitches in a single strand of Rajmahal 379.

Cut out and assemble the pansies (see diagram 5). Add a few straight stitches and a French knot in the centre with Kacoonda fine wool 17, before attaching the pansies to the background of the left half-heart. Work the two pansy bud edges in blanket stitch with Kacoonda fine wool 108. Attach to the background, straight stitch the calyx and stems in Gumnut Daisies 628.

Work the five pansy leaves in the same manner as the clematis leaves in Gumnut Daisies 629. Stitch the veins in Rajmahal 65. Attach the leaves in position on the left half-heart, and stem-stitch the stems in Rajmahal 65.

Carnations

Divide the 1 ¼ in (35 mm) white and rose painted silk ribbon into three pieces. Run a line of running stitches through the centre of each ribbon piece (see diagram 6 below). Pull the ribbon into a tight ruffle and stitch the centre of the gathering firmly. Position on the background of the right half-heart and stitch into place. Ribbon-stitch a calyx below each flower in Kacoonda 7 mm silk ribbon 104, then twist two stems of 4 mm Kacoonda 104 silk ribbon and stitch them below the calyxes. Using the same ribbon, work ribbon-stitch leaves on the stems as in the photograph.

Diagram 6 Carnation

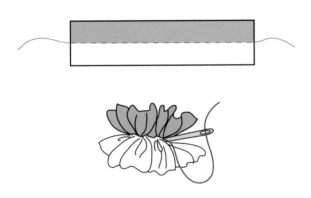

Butterfly

Cut out the butterfly from the template in ruby organza, tack in place onto the background of the left heart. Following the stitching diagram, work straight stitches over the butterfly in 2 strands of Rajmahal 379. For the body, work several straight stitches, then whip them, in Kreinik metallic 093. Add two pistil stitches for the antennae. Take out the tacking stitches.

Forget-me-nots

Work 5 single-wrap French knots in Kacoonda thick silk 3C for each flower, with 1 double-wrap French knot in 2 strands of Anchor Marlitt 1076 for the centres. The stems in straight stitch, and the leaves in lazy daisy stitch, are worked in a single strand of Gumnut Buds 647. Scatter these flowers around the background of the two half-hearts following the flower placement diagram.

Organza butterfly template

for left half-heart
cut 1 (right side up) in ruby organza

Butterfly stitching diagram

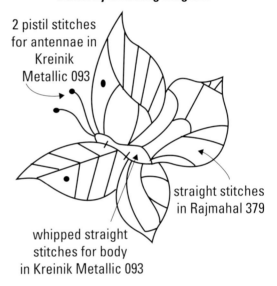

2 pistil stitches for antennae in Kreinik Metallic 093

straight stitches in Rajmahal 379

whipped straight stitches for body in Kreinik Metallic 093

Making up

Cut out the pairs of half-hearts, then with right sides facing work a line of hand-stitching along the seam line (see diagram on next page), making sure you do not catch the three-dimensional work into the seam. Leave an opening large enough to carefully turn the work through to the right side. Position the work on a towel, then press carefully with a steam iron, working the tip of the iron lightly between the flowers and leaves to press the edges of the heart as crisply as possible, then slip-stitch the openings closed.

Position the half-hearts carefully over the ruby sateen heart already stitched onto the background linen. Catch the sides of the half-hearts to the background and the ruby sateen heart with neat slip stitches.

Diagram 7 Making up heart

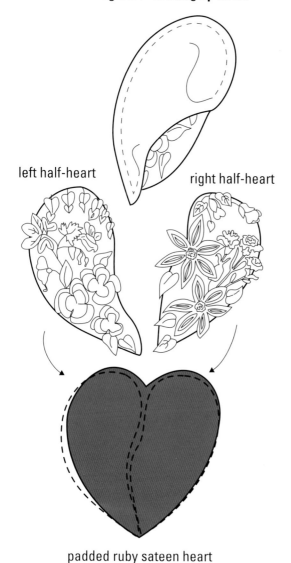

left half-heart

right half-heart

padded ruby sateen heart

Organza butterfly cloud

Trace the 15 butterfly outlines from the template onto the 10 x 12 inch (25 x 30 cm) piece of ruby organza with the water-erasable pen. Secure the fabric in an embroidery hoop large enough to work all the butterflies without repositioning the fabric.

Using the dark ruby machine thread, machine-stitch a narrow dense zigzag stitch along the outlines of the butterflies. Cut out the shapes, fold them in half and stitch the butterflies onto the background according to the placement chart. Straight-stitch the bodies, and pistil-stitch the antennae, with Kreinik metallic thread 093.

Finishing

Finally, catch the tips of the clematis petals into place with machine thread. Remove tacking thread from the background fabric. Remove any traces of blue pen with cold water. Lightly steam-press the background to remove any wrinkles, taking care not to damage your work. Take the finished piece to a professional framer.

Butterfly cloud placement
Position butterflies on background above heart.

Butterfly cloud template
Trace butterflies onto deep ruby organza (do not cut
out until all outlines have been zigzag machine
stitched with the dark ruby machine thread).

Treasured Heart
Kaylene Evans

*K*ay was introduced to embroidery ten years ago by a close friend and has since developed a passion for fine embroidery and memorabilia design. Kay finds inspiration for her work in many places, including gardens and nature, and enjoys collecting old and beautiful objects and fabrics to use in her work.

Over time her hobby has turned into a business that she operates from the family farm near Stawell in Victoria. Originally her business focused on designing and embroidering original pieces and making these into mail order embroidery kits. The first few years of business saw all hands on deck with her husband Peter and two children all standing around the billiard table helping to assemble kits.

Later, Kay and Peter travelled extensively throughout Australia, attending needlework and craft shows and running workshops. 'Having seen my work and editorials in magazines, people knew us by the time they met us on our stand; they treated us like old friends and became wonderful ongoing customers who still catch up with us just to say hello.'

Recently, however, Kay has decided to focus her attention on writing. She regularly contributes projects to popular needlework and craft magazines and has published three embroidery books.

Kay believes in supporting anything that benefits the good and well-being of others and was delighted to participate in *Embroidery from the Heart*. She felt a particular link with this project because a few years ago, at the age of 45, her brother Gary died from a heart attack.

Kay has created a heart full of buttons, beads, ribbon work and fine embroidery. 'After years of experimenting and learning from others these styles of work have become my favourites—especially when combined.'

Kaylene may be contacted at: RMB 4102, Stawell Vic 3380, phone/fax (03) 5359 8290

This piece is designed purely as an 'inspirational piece', as I am fully aware that not all readers will be able to access the same sorts of treasures that I have used. Many treasured finds may be incorporated into the design, such as old or new costume jewellery, old or new buttons, charms, badges and so on.

For those who are not skilled ribbon rose makers, you can buy lovely ready-made roses and other flowers that would suit your piece beautifully. You can also dye purchased flowers in tea or coffee and then add a little fabric or folk art paint (plus textile medium) to the centre of the flower, and finish off with a touch of colour around the outer edges, to achieve just the effect you want.

I have intentionally written the following instructions to allow readers to follow their own personal tastes and preferences. Use the photo as your main guide for the placement of flower buds, buttons, charms etc.

Stitches used: Back stitch, bullion stitch, feather stitch, folded ribbon rosebuds.

MATERIALS REQUIRED

background fabric, approximately 20 inches (50 cm) square (I used a light gold watermark curtaining fabric)
strengthening fabric (e.g. calico), approximately 20 inches (50 cm) square
plastic for template
assortment of old and new buttons, some flat, some with shank (the shanked buttons will sit above flat buttons beautifully)
assortment of seed beads and other small beads (for filling in tiny spaces)
heart charm for centre of design
⅝ inch (15 mm) Old Gold or Antique Gold double satin ribbon for rosebuds (or silk ribbon in colour of your choice)
4 small cream ready-made roses
stranded thread:
green for feather stitch at base of heart
colour of your choice for rosebuds surrounding feather stitch
needles:
#10 straw for rosebuds
#10 crewel for feather stich
invisible thread, or thread matching the treasures, for stitching everything into place (no glue should be used in this project)

Preparation

If you are using old bits and pieces, clean them thoroughly before using—unless, of course, you love the charming patina of old pieces. I love using sentimental and special treasures but I do not recommend the use of very expensive pieces (such as diamond rings!). This work is a form of embellished and decorative embroidery, not a form of preservation.

The use of a hoop is optional, although it will help to keep the fabric taut and help to prevent the puckering which can occur when stitching so many pieces onto fabric. Choose a size that allows you freedom and comfort while working.

Lay calico behind the background fabric and tack the two pieces together. Work from the centre to each corner, then from the centre to each side, and finally from the centre to the top and bottom of the fabric. Tacking in this sequence will help keep both pieces even.

Diagram 1

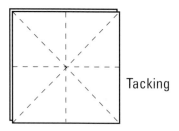

Tacking

Use a photocopier to enlarge or reduce the heart to the size you want. Trace the outline of the heart onto the template plastic, cut out the heart shape and position the template on the centre of the background fabric. Using a soft lead pencil gently draw around the template outline.

Make a few small folded ribbon roses or rosebuds (whichever you prefer) in gold or your preferred colour.

I made two medium rosebuds, one small one and two extra small ones. Remember that you can also use ready-made flowers—these are lovely when incorporated into a design with your own hand-made flowers. I used four ready-made roses (dyed in coffee with their centres and outer petals coloured in dark pink).

Folded ribbon rosebud

Fold ribbon over approximately at a
right angle, leaving a small tail

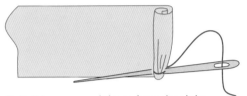

Roll ribbon several times from the right
until the fold is covered, stitching
through each layer to secure

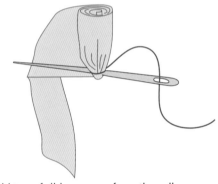

Fold top of ribbon away from the roll;
keep rolling until fold is covered,
continuing to securely stitch each layer;
repeat until rose is required size

For a small rosebud, make only
two or three rolls

Positioning the treasures

Now spend time arranging your bits and pieces—
think of it as a jigsaw puzzle, and leave it for a
while. When you come back to it, rearrange it if
needed. Keep doing this until it all comes together.
This can be a very relaxing pastime.

Where you choose to use buttons, stitch on any
flat ones first, slightly overlapping them if

necessary. Stitch shanked buttons in between the
gaps. Catch down each button at the back of work
with a couple of tiny back stiches. Don't worry
about any gaps that might be left at this stage.

I began working my design at the centre top of
the heart, worked just over halfway down the right
side and then repeated the same order (as best as I
could) down the left side. I stitched on three
rosebuds at the centre top and then proceeded to
stitch on flat buttons around the top curve of heart
and down the right side. I added shanked buttons
in the tiny gaps between the flat buttons (as
mentioned above), and tucked in a couple of
ready-made roses. Working further down the side,
I stitched on another rosebud and finished off with
a flower-shaped button and a couple of mauve
tulip-shaped beads. I then tried to work the left-
hand side to correspond with the right side. Don't
let yourself get frustrated doing this—it does not
matter if the two sides are not perfectly matched,
for remember this heart is hand-worked with love.

Embroidery

I then embroidered feather stitch in 2 strands of
green from the finish of the button work to the
bottom tip of the heart, doing the same on both
sides, then a tiny bullion rosebud (using 1 strand
of thread) at the tip of each feather stitch.

Bullion rosebud

Using #10 straw needle and 1 strand
of thread, embroider two 10-wrap
bullions close together

With #10 crewel needle and 1 or 2 strands
of green thread, surround the bullions
with a fly stitch

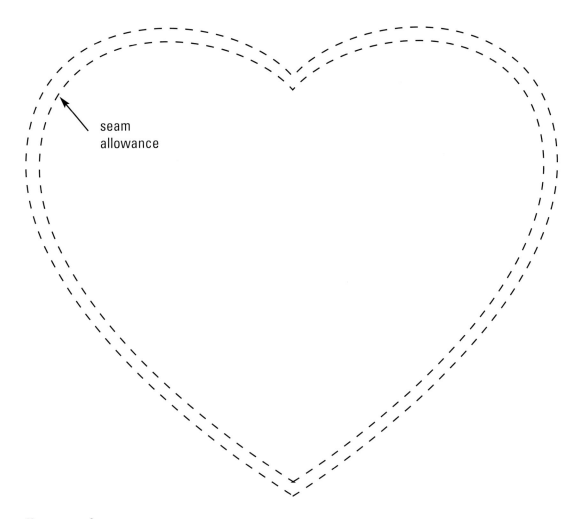

seam
allowance

Heart template
reduce or enlarge to required size

Finishing

To finish off I filled in any little gaps with 3 mm and 4 mm matt gold beads, and filled in any button holes left showing with tiny seed beads. Lastly, I added the antique gold brass heart underneath the roses at the top, and carefully removed the tacking.

Have your work professionally framed. Remember that dimensional work such as this requires a box frame.

Lace and Latticework
Helen Dafter

*H*elen, who was taught to stitch by her grandmother even before she went to school, specialises in silk ribbon embroidery with hand-painted backgrounds. One of the reasons ribbon embroidery is her favourite is because she enjoys the fact that beautiful results can be achieved quickly.

Helen runs a mail order business distributing her embroidery kits and patterns. She regularly publishes her embroidery projects in the major craft magazines and is the author of five embroidery books. She is kept busy travelling to the major craft shows and teaching, lecturing and demonstrating her work in Australia and overseas.

Helen's other interests include gardening, reading and travelling. She also loves to relax by doing colourwash patchwork which she says is like 'painting with fabric'.

Helen was honoured to be involved in *Embroidery from the Heart*, seeing it as a perfect opportunity to use her skills in a unique way to further the work of the Heart Foundation.

Helen chose to use silk ribbon, beads and hand-dyed lace motifs in her favourite shades of blue and lemon to create a heart design which is both fresh and pretty with a touch of nostalgia. The butterfly in her design represents a new life.

Helen may be contacted at: RMB 5430, The Ridgeway, Holgate NSW 2550,
phone/fax (02) 4367 7694
e-mail: helen@helendafter.com.au

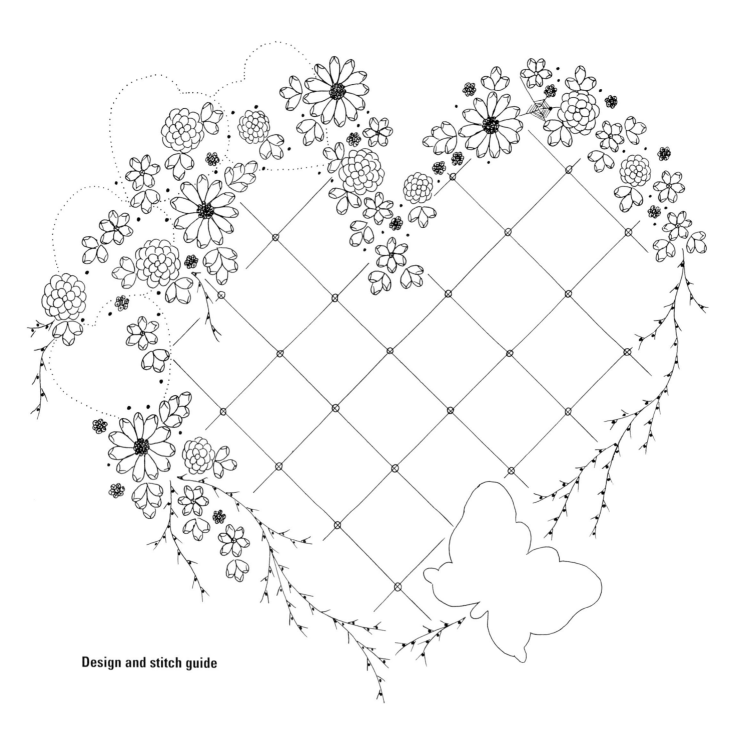

Design and stitch guide

Stitches used: Feather stitch, French knot, ribbon stitch, spider web/woven rose, stem stitch, straight stitch.

MATERIALS REQUIRED

moiré taffeta, pale blue, 14 inches (35 cm) square
iron-on interfacing such as Armor Weft (optional)
7 mm YLI silk ribbon: 3 ¼ yd (3m) #5 (Very Pale Pink)
4 mm YLI silk ribbon:
   4 ⅓ yd (4 m) #13 (Pale Lemon)
   3 ⅓ yd (3 m) #1 (Antique White), #15 (Bright Yellow), #178 (Light Grape)
   2 ¼ yd (2 m) #20 (Medium Grass Green), #31 (Light Apple Green), #72 (Dark Jungle Green), #125 (Light Blue)
   1 ¼ yd (1 m) #32 (Light Blue Green)
Rajmahal Stranded Art Silk: #221 (Pastel Grey), #29 (Charcoal)
Madeira Metallic Machine Thread, silver
4 lace heart motifs (see note)
1 lace butterfly motif (see note)
22 x ⅛ inch (3 mm) seed pearls
pale blue seed beads
2 inch (5 cm) ecru needle-run edging lace, 1.5 m (1 ½ yd)
fine-tip water-erasable fabric marking pen
12 inch (30 cm) embroidery hoop
needles:
   chenille #18 for silk ribbon
   crewel #9 for stranded thread

(**Note**: The lace motifs were hand-dyed using cold-water dyes. They were wet when the dye was applied to allow the colours to blend. Colours used included pink, mauve and blue.)

If desired, iron the interfacing to the back of the moiré taffeta. This is not essential but does give additional stability to the fabric and also allows the ends of the silk ribbon to be buried between the two layers to eliminate the need to stitch down 'loose' ends.

Trace the heart template onto card, cut out and position in the middle of the fabric. Trace around the template with the fabric marking pen. Place the fabric in the hoop after tracing the design.

Position the four lace heart motifs at the top left-hand side of the heart, overlapping them as shown on the pattern, and pin in place. Position the butterfly and pin in place. Using a single strand of

Rajmahal 221, and tiny straight stiches, sew all the motifs in place.

Refer to the pattern diagram and mark in the position of the large white daisies and the large pink roses. It will not detract from the design if they are not in exactly the same position as on the pattern sheet, as the smaller flowers can be adjusted to fill in the spaces.

Follow the chart below to complete the embroidery.

Flower	Ribbon/thread	Stitch
Large pink roses		
petals	YLI 5 (7 mm)	spider web/woven rose
leaves	YLI 32 (4 mm)	ribbon stitch

White daisies		
centres	YLI 15 (4 mm)	French knots
petals	YLI 1 (4 mm)	ribbon stitch
leaves	YLI 72 (4 mm)	ribbon stitch

Small mauve roses		
petals	YLI 178 (4 mm)	spider web/woven rose
leaves	YLI 20 (4 mm)	ribbon stitch

Heart template
Enlarge at 143% on a photocopier

Lemon daisies

centres	YLI 15 (4 mm)	French knot
petals	YLI 13 (4 mm)	ribbon stitch
leaves	YLI 31 (4 mm)	ribbon stitch

Forget-me-nots

centres	YLI 15 (4 mm)	French knot
petals	YLI 125 (4 mm)	French knot

Latticework

lattice	Rajmahal 221	stem stitch
		x 2 strands

3 mm seed pearl sewn at each intersection

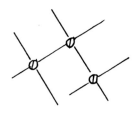

Bead foliage

stems	Rajmahal 221	feather stitch
and leaves		x 2 strands

pale blue seed bead sewn in each V formed by the feather stitch

Spider and web

web	Madeira silver	straight stitch
spider	Rajmahal 29	French knot
		x 2 strands

Once the embroidery is completed, use a cotton bud dipped in cold water to remove any marks still visible from the fabric marking pen. Take care with the water near the lace motifs, as some dyes may run.

The embroidery was professionally framed with a double matt mount. The needle-run lace was positioned with mitred corners and the scallops matching before the gilt frame and glass were put in place.

Redwork: A Work of Heart!
Christine Book

Christine has been embroidering since she was five years old and quilting since she was fourteen! She loves the naïve country look, combining embroidery and patchwork in her work.

Over the past few years she has developed a passion for redwork, a style of embroidery that peaked in popularity at the turn of the nineteenth century and is currently enjoying a revival. Christine says she loves its graphic qualities and how easy it is to take along with you anywhere.

Redwork or outline embroidery was traditionally worked on household linen: napkins, tea towels, dresser scarves and pillow shams. Redwork also appears frequently on old quilts—often summer coverlets which contain no batting.

Along with a partner Christine runs Christine Book Designs, publishing patterns for quilters. In 1999 they published their first book, *Stitched Verse*. That was followed in 2001 by *Stitched Vintage*, and *Stitched in Time for Christmas* appeared in 2002. The partners are kept busy publishing regular newsletters to help keep patchworkers, quilters and stitchers in touch.

Christine loved the thought of participating in *Embroidery from the Heart* and being able to help such a worthwhile cause through doing what she loves best—being creative! 'Heart motifs always feature in my designs. I've included a heart in everything I have created.'

Christine created an achievable redwork embroidery design featuring simple heart motifs and a little appliquéd heart pocket with a message inside. Her message to you is 'Follow your heart!'

Christine may be contacted at: PO Box 60, Pendle Hill NSW 2145,
phone/fax (02) 9625 5368
(Photo of Christine by Sue Stubbs/Homespun)

MATTERS OF THE HEART
Christine Book 2001

Tracing pattern
Enlarge at 143% on a photocopier

pocket

MATTERS OF THE HEART

Stitches used: Back stitch, French knot, Pekinese stitch.

MATERIALS REQUIRED

22 x 24 inches (55 x 60 cm) white cotton/linen fabric (e.g. Sienna linen, a cotton/linen blend fabric similar in weight and texture to Osnaburg, or a quality cotton homespun)

DMC Perle 8 threads:
　　#115 variegated reds and black
　　#498 light burgundy
　　#815 dark burgundy

embroidery hoop, 15 cm (6 inches) fits comfortably in the hand

Piecemakers #7 embroidery needles and appliqué needles

Pigma Micron 01 pen, red or brown, for transferring design onto fabric

scraps of red/burgundy cotton print fabrics (a selection of about 18 prints), cut into short strips 2 ½ inches (6.5 cm) wide

red cotton for appliqué and machine piecing

small piece of paper for message

general sewing supplies (pins, scissors, sewing machine, etc.)

Finished size

Redwork design (hearts and words) 16 ⅛ x 10 ¼ inches (41 x 26 cm)

Frame size of your choice to be determined when work completed

Tracing the design

Using a light source, such as a glass window or light box, trace the design from the pattern onto the centre of your fabric. I trace with a fine-point Pigma pen and use a light touch. If possible use a pen the same colour as the embroidery thread you will be using (for example, red pen, red thread). To prevent the fabric moving around while tracing, pin to the pattern in several places.

Embroidery

Work embroidery. Placing your work in an embroidery hoop helps to keep the tension even.

1. Hearts and vine border: even back stitch in perle 115.
2. Straight line border: Pekinese stitch in perle 498.
3. Dividing lines inside frame: back stitch and 1-wrap French knots in perle 498.
4. Heart motifs: back stitch and 1-wrap French knots in perle 815.
5. Words: back stitch in perle 498.

Press embroidery flat using a hot steam iron, working only on the back.

Appliqué pocket

Select a scrap of burgundy print fabric about 4 x 8 inches (10 x 20 cm). Halve the fabric so that you have two 4 inch (10 cm) squares. Make a cardboard template of the heart shape for pocket. Using pencil, trace the heart shape onto the wrong side of one of the fabric squares. Place the two squares right side together and machine, using a short stitch, on the pencil line, pivoting at the heart's points. Trim seam allowance to about ⅛ inch (3 mm), clip points and curves. Make a small slit in one layer of the fabric and turn through to the right side through the slit, gently pushing out the points and curves. Using a thread to match the fabric, quilt an even running stitch around the heart about ⅛ inch (3 mm) in from the edge.

Appliqué your heart pocket in position using a thread to match and small blind-hemming stitches. Start at the top of the heart on the left-hand side and finish at the top of the heart on the right hand side. Leave the indent open—this forms the pocket.

Patchwork border

The border is pieced randomly from the selection of red/burgundy cotton print fabrics in pieces 2 ½ inches (6.5 cm) wide, ranging in length from 2 to 5 inches (5 to 12 cm). The border is constructed in log cabin patchwork fashion—top border, right-hand side, bottom and lastly left-hand side.

Lay out your 2 ½ inch (6.5 cm) wide strips for each side in a pleasing arrangement. Machine piece the strips together to form 'logs' long enough to cover each side. With the pieced log right sides together with the embroidered panel, machine stitch along the log's length. Flip the log open and press flat with hot iron. Continue in this 'stitch and flip' manner until logs have been added on each side. Note each new log covers the raw end of the previous log. Tack the raw edges down to ensure that this patchwork log cabin border sits flat.

The border is pieced onto the linen background panel so that enough fabric remains around the embroidery to enable the work to be framed.

Note: Should you wish to make up this design into a small wall quilt, cut the embroidery down to the desired size, then add the pieced log cabin border. Quilt as desired and finish with a binding.

Message

Don't forget to include a little message, in your best handwriting, on a piece of paper in the heart pocket—perhaps something like 'Follow your heart', 'Bless this home with happy hearts' or 'Busy hands, happy hearts'.

My Heart Blooms
in My Garden
Donna Cumming
and Teena Volta

*D*onna and Teena are not only sisters but business partners as well. Their business, Attic Crafts, is a needlework and patchwork speciality store located in Bendigo, Victoria, offering equipment, supplies and classes in embroidery and patchwork.

As children they loved to play with offcuts of fabric, buttons, ribbons and lace used by their mother, a talented dressmaker. They love embroidery and favour a relaxed and approachable attitude to it. 'We encourage our students to take pleasure in creating and not let themselves get too worried about rules because, after all, embroidery is meant to be fun.'

Donna and Teena have written four books on embroidery and have had numerous articles published in embroidery magazines. They also visit a number of craft shows each year to meet their customers and promote their embroidery kits and other products.

Donna and Teena agreed to participate in *Embroidery from the Heart* because 'heart disease affects many families, including ours, and it is a chance to give back something to the community that has supported us'.

As the styles they work in vary from naive country to elegant Victoriana, the hardest part was deciding what style to embroider. Donna and Teena chose to create this crazy heart which combines patchwork, painted backgrounds and thread and ribbon embroidery, with a touch of the naive look in the verse.

Donna and Teena may be contacted at: Attic Crafts, 98 Queen Street, Bendigo Vic 3550, phone (03) 5441 7333, fax (03) 5443 5351

Stitches used: Back stitch, bullion stitch, chain stitch, feather stitch, fly stitch, French knot, herringbone stitch, lazy daisy buttonhole, loop stitch, ribbon stitch, stem stitch, straight stitch, twirled rose

MATERIALS REQUIRED

22 inch (55 cm) square beige background fabric
13 inch (32 cm) square quilter's muslin (or good quality calico), plus a small piece to paint
scraps of print fabrics in dusky pinks, blues and custard yellow
DMC stranded cottons: #676, 3752, 739, 224, 3053
DMC perle 8: #676, 932, 224
1 pkt Petals hand-dyed 4 mm silk ribbon, Rosemary
YLI 4 mm silk ribbon:
  1 ¼ yd (1 m) #125 Dusky Blue
  3 ⅓ yd (3 m) #90 Light Blue
  2 ¼ yd (2 m) #35 Pale Old Gold
  1 ¼ yd (1 m) #156 Cream
  2 ¼ yd (2 m) #110 Pink
1 pkt each Mill Hill glass seed beads:
  00161 Clear Crystal
  00123 Cream
  62046 (frosted) Cornflower Blue
  62033 (frosted) Pale Pink
  70123 (small bugle) Cream
1 each Mill Hill Glass Treasures (frosted charms, can substitute other charms if desired):
  12074 heart
  12052 bird
  12118 flower
DMC stranded silver metallic thread
6 x ⅜ inch (10 mm) pearl buttons
needles:
  straw (milliner's) #8 and #3
  crewel (embroidery) #8
  chenille #22
  beading
embroidery hoop, 10 or 12 inch (24 or 30 cm)
Staedtler Lumocolor pen 313 (brown)
Jo Sonja acrylic paints:
  Green Oxide
  Raw Umber
  paintbrush

Method

Basket

Using the Lumocolor pen, trace the basket design onto the small piece of quilter's muslin. Dilute the paint to a wash and paint in the basket and ground beneath in Raw Umber. Dry. Shade the basket by repainting the required areas with the same paint mixture. Dry. Paint in a wash of Green Oxide for the leaves. Dry and iron.

Crazy patchwork

The crazy patchwork is stitched onto a base cloth of quilter's muslin. I prefer to use a hoop to try to prevent puckering. Fold under at least ¼ inch (5 mm) seams on all visible sides. Sides that are overlapped do not need a seam. Start off-centre with a five-sided shape. Pin all pieces in place. You may need to play around with this to get a pleasing result. Do not try to exactly duplicate what we have done as this will make life difficult! Curves are a nice change to straight lines. Build an area slightly larger than the heart shape. Tack all pieces into position, when you are happy with the result. Tack the heart shape around the outline.

Seams

Embroider along the edges of the pieces with seams. This is what will hold it together so make sure that you stitch through to the quilter's muslin. Unless I am making a feature, such as the butterflies, I embroider with a matching colour stranded cotton (2 strands). See below for seam ideas—but in general, any closely embroidered stitches will be fine. When all seams are embroidered, remove tacking stitches (except from heart outline).

Tracing pattern

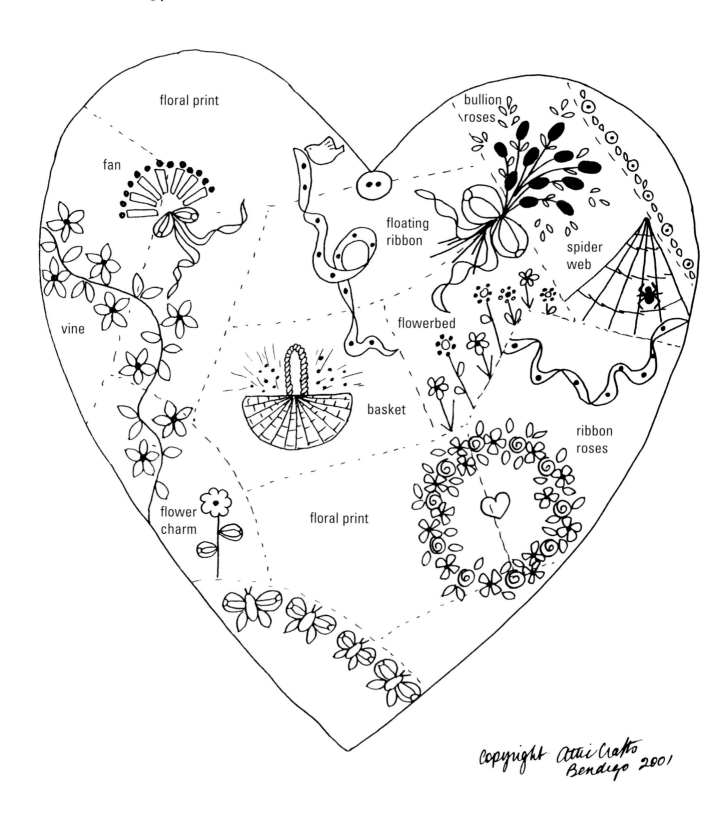

floral print

bullion roses

fan

floating ribbon

spider web

vine

flowerbed

basket

ribbon roses

flower charm

floral print

Suggestions for seam embroidery

Buttonhole stitch, chain stitch, fly stitch (both horizontal and vertical), herringbone stitch, feather stitch.

Chain stitch variations

Bead flowers

Rosettes: Place two pins like a cross, picking up a very small amount of fabric. Wrap 2 strands of thread around and around under the pins. Catch, with the same thread, in the four areas between the pins (this holds the thread). Stitch a bead in the centre, and add lazy daisy leaves.

Butterflies: Using silk ribbon, make lazy daisy stitches for the upper wings. Stitch a straight stitch body and lower wings in ribbon stitch. Work straight stitch, in 2 strands of thread, for the feelers. Vary the colours.

copyright Attic Crafts
Bendigo 2001

Lettering template
Enlarge at 154% on a photocopier

Embellish the crazy patchwork panel with embroidery (see main diagram for details). I usually work in a free-flowing manner so the embroidery will run over at least two blocks. If the motifs are embroidered only inside each section, they look a little stiff.

Fill the basket with French knots in 2 strands of all the stranded threads.

Bullion roses

Stitch, with 2 strands of pink thread, a bunch of bullion roses. Each rosebud is three bullion stitches with approximately 10 wraps for each one. Stems are 2 strands of green in stem stitch. Leaves are lazy daisy in the same thread. The bow is dusky blue silk ribbon. Stitch two lazy daisy loops and twisted, long straight stitches for the tails. Catch them into position (in several places) with 1 strand of matching thread.

Ribbon roses

Position five pink and five old gold ribbon twirled roses to make the wreath, alternating them. Fill the gaps in between with one or two loop stitch flowers (four petals) in light blue 90 ribbon. Stitch pink beads in the centres of these flowers. Scatter ribbon stitch leaves around and in any gaps in the Petals ribbon. Sew the heart charm in the centre.

Vine

Meander a vine in 2 strands of green thread (stem stitch). On each side of the vine embroider ribbon stitch flowers (five petals) using pink and old gold ribbons, and stitch blue beads in the centres. Stitch ribbon stitch leaves, in Petals ribbon, along the stem.

Flower bed

Along one of the seams plant a flower bed of alternating thread and bead flowers. The blue lazy daisy flowers have five petals and a cream bead centre, and their straight stitch leaves and stems are worked in 2 strands of green thread. The bead flowers have a blue bead centre surrounded by pink bead petals, with straight stitch stems and lazy daisy leaves worked in 2 strands of green thread. Vary the heights of the flowers.

Ribbon

Trail one or two lengths of old gold ribbon across the patchwork, making it twist and curl. Hold the ribbon in place with blue and pink beads spaced along its length. Stitch the bird charm to one end.

Flower charm

Embroider a stem in 2 strands of green stem stitch. Stitch the flower charm to the top of the stem, and give it a pink bead centre. Stitch lazy daisy leaves in Petals ribbon on each side.

Spider web

Use 2 stands of metallic silver to embroider the spider web in long straight stitches in a triangle shape (like a tepee). Stitch across these with a long, messy stem stitch in the same thread. The spider's body is two crystal beads. Work the straight stitch legs with the same silver thread.

Fan

The bugle beads make the ribs of the fan. Stitch cream beads at the tip of each bugle bead and between them, at the top of the gap between the ribs. Using 2 strands of cream thread, work straight stitches to continue the ribs, connecting at the bottom centre. Work a smaller version of the bow on the rosebuds in cream ribbon.

When all embroidery is complete, cut out the heart shape, allowing an extra $\frac{3}{8}$ inch (10 mm) for seams. Turn under the seams and appliqué onto the beige background fabric.

Lettering

Trace the lettering around the heart shape onto the background fabric from the lettering template. Work this in perle 8 blue, using back stitch. Position a French knot (double wrap) in the same thread at the tips of each letter. The small heart at the end is worked in satin stitch in the same thread, and outlined in back stitch. The flowers have lazy daisy petals and a pearl button for a centre; they are worked in perle 8, either pink or old gold. Stitch the buttons on with perle 8 in old gold.

The finished work was professionally mounted in a box frame.

Friendship Heart
Bernadette Janson

Bernadette Janson fell in love with embroidery at the age of nine and has been embroidering for over 20 years. She has a particular interest in smocking, enjoys designing and teaches from her studio in Beecroft in Sydney's leafy northern suburbs. Bernadette has had several pieces published in embroidery magazines.

Bernadette initiated the project *Embroidery from the Heart* after her close friend Kerry Teulan died unexpectedly of a heart attack at the age of 37. Bernadette wanted to do something to commemorate her life and let people know about the dangers of heart disease. 'As hearts are often featured in embroidery design I thought they would be an appropriate theme for this project.'

Bernadette's piece was inspired by the qualities of friendship and everything in it has a purpose and a reason for being there. Bernadette used very simple materials and stitches to signify the generation of something beautiful from humble beginnings, and a diverse range of elements—paint, thread and glass—to celebrate life's complexity. The imperfect shapes suggest that perfection is not necessary to produce true beauty.

'The trailing vine represents growth and change; the gold filament is for richness; the depth of colour is for warmth; and the central glass heart is for love.'

Bernadette may be contacted at: 2 Naluara Close, Beecroft NSW 2119,
phone (02) 9875 5489
e-mail: jansonb@bigpond.com.au

Pattern diagram and stencil outline

Stitches used: Back stitch, bullion stitch, chain stitch, detached chain stitch, fly stitch, French knot, granitos, straight stitch, whip stitch.

20 inches (50 cm) square of seeded homespun fabric
DMC stranded threads:
> *3013 Light Khaki Green*
> *3012 Medium Khaki Green*
> *3011 Dark Khaki Green*
> *3802 Very Dark Antique Mauve*
> *3726 Dark Antique Mauve*
> *730 Very Dark Olive Green*
> *3828 Hazelnut Brown*
> *3740 Dark Antique Violet*
> *3861 Light Cocoa*
> *794 Dark Steel Grey*

Mill Hill glass beads 03031 and 00367
Mill Hill glass treasures 12075
Madeira Glisten Gloss 03
4 mm silk ribbon (Aubergine)
Jo Sonja paints:
> *Plum Pink*
> *Rich Gold*

textile medium
stencil brush
fine liner brush 00
water-soluble marking pen
fine firm cardboard
sharp scalpel or craft knife

Preparation

Pre-wash the fabric and press it before transferring the design using the water-soluble marker. You may wish to place the fabric in an embroidery hoop, but this is not essential.

Cut a stencil for the sawtooth border from the cardboard.

Painted border

Tape the stencil into position on the fabric, lining it up with the design markings. Blend each of the paints with textile medium according to manufacturer's instructions before applying to the fabric. Using the stencil brush loaded with Plum Pink, dab the excess paint onto a paper towel and pounce the paint onto the stencil area to give the desired coverage. Gently remove the stencil and allow to dry. Take the fine liner brush, load

sparingly with Rich Gold and, starting at a corner, paint the fine stripe on each side of the frame, keeping the width as even as possible. Outline the peaks of the teeth with gold. Allow to dry. Cover fabric with a clean cloth and press with a dry iron to set the paint.

Embroidery

All embroidery is worked in 2 strands unless otherwise stated. Use the photograph as a guide.

Outer vine border

Work the vine in chain stitch in DMC 3013 and whip with a single strand of Madeira Glisten Gloss 03.

Work 3-stitch granitos in DMC 3012 for the leaves, surrounded by detached chain stitch in a single strand of Madeira Glisten Gloss 03 along either side of the vine.

Work the rosebuds with two bullions of 9 wraps in DMC 3802. Attach the rosebuds to the stem with a fly stitch in DMC 3012, then work a stamen on each rosebud with single-strand straight stitch in the same thread.

Verse

Back-stitch the verse in DMC 3726.

Corners

Work the heart in back stitch with a single strand of DMC 730. Embroider three bullion roses in each corner, the inners with two 7-wrap bullions in DMC 3802, the outers with two or three 7-wrap bullions in DMC 3726.

Work the detached chain leaves and French knots in DMC 730.

Attach three seed beads (Mill Hill 00367) at the top of the heart, and two or three beads among each group of roses.

Heart and inner square of painted border

Embroider the inner square of the painted border in chain stitch in 4 strands of DMC 3828. Whip the chain stitch with a single strand of Madeira Glisten Gloss 03.

Repeat this technique to outline the heart.

Vine within border

Work a chain-stitch vine in a single strand of DMC 3011. Work leaves along either side of the vine in 3-stitch granitos in DMC 3013 and surround each leaf with detached chain in DMC 3011.

Inside heart

Work the roses with inners of two 8-wrap bullions in DMC 3802 and outers of two or three 11-wrap bullions in DMC 3726. Surround the roses with leaves in DMC 3011.

Embroider the wisteria in colonial knots using the darker DMC 3740 towards the top and the lighter DMC 3861 below, adding a few dark knots among the light and a few light knots among the dark. Stitch some Mill Hill glass beads 03031 among the knots.

Work the wisteria leaves in 3 or 4-stitch granitos in 3 strands of DMC 730, and surround with a detached chain in the same thread.

Work the lavender in detached chain, following the diagram, in DMC 414.

Fill the spaces in the heart with detached chain leaves and French knots in DMC 3011, adding Mill Hill glass beads 00376 randomly between the flowers and leaves.

Inner garland

Work the chain-stitch oval with a single strand of DMC 3013. Using DMC 730, work leaves of 3-stitch granitos evenly around the oval, both inside and out. Surround each leaf with a detached chain in a single strand of Madeira Glisten Gloss 03.

Glass heart and bow

Stitch the glass heart to the top of the inner garland so that it lies flat. Tie a length of the silk ribbon into a bow, leaving enough to trail either side of the inner garland. Pin the ribbon into the desired position and stitch, using a single strand of DMC 3861.

Have the finished work professionally mounted in a deep frame.

Valentine Roses
Jane Ellis

*J*ane has always been 'crafty', enjoying knitting, smocking and paper tole, but when she saw Victorian style embroidery for the first time she knew immediately that it would be her main focus—and it quickly came to occupy all her spare time.

Working from home, Jane finds inspiration from her picturesque gardens with beautiful roses and colourful flowerbeds. She loves working with hand-dyed silk ribbon and often dyes her own when she wants a particular colour to complement the images used in her work.

Jane has been teaching embroidery for over four years and runs her own business from home, teaching classes specialising in Judith & Kathryn silk prints, urns and embroidery shapes. Her work regularly appears in embroidery publications and Judith & Kathryn books and is displayed at major craft fairs throughout Australia and overseas.

Having lost her father to undiagnosed heart problems at the age of 53 when she was only 17 years old, Jane was particularly pleased to have the opportunity to help raise awareness and funds for the Heart Foundation.

For *Embroidery from the Heart*, Jane has created 'Valentine Roses', a Judith & Kathryn silk print embellished with silk ribbon and thread embroidery, ribbon roses and beads. The delicate silk print heart is brought to life as a three-dimensional heirloom piece. Jane has dedicated this piece to the memory of her father, Robert Cornelus Elkson (nee Elkhuizen), who instilled in her the need for excellence, perfection and attention to detail.

Jane may be contacted at: Jane's Ribbon Roses, 5 Vaucluse Drive, Happy Valley SA 5159, phone/fax (08) 8381 3525 www.judithandkathryn.com
e-mail: janesrr@senet.com.au

Stitches used: French knot, lazy daisy stitch, loop stitch, ribbon stitch, rolled ribbon roses, straight stitch, twisted straight stitch.

Note: Where the silk ribbons specified are not readily available you can substitute other brands using the photograph as a colour guide.

MATERIALS REQUIRED

Judith & Kathryn silk print 'Rose Heart Wreath',
   WR03-M
Jane's Hand Dyed 13 mm silk ribbon:
   50 cm Hand-Dyed Rose Pink
   60 cm Hand-Dyed Cornsilk
Jane's Hand Dyed 7 mm silk ribbon:
   3 m Hand-Dyed Rose Pink
   1 m Hand-Dyed Cornsilk
   2 m Hand-Dyed Fern Green
   1 m YLI #156 Cream
Jane's Hand Dyed 4 mm silk ribbon:
   2 m Hand-Dyed Olivine
   1 m Hand-Dyed Rose Pink
   1 m YLI #156 Cream
Rajmahal silk thread, Gold 45
DMC stranded cotton:
   932 Blue
   3726 Deep Pink
   9520 Dark Green
   523 Light Green
Maria George size 11/0 embroidery beads 9114
   Cream
needles
   sharps #8, #10
   beading
   chenille #18, #20

Press all the silk ribbons to remove any creases in readiness for embroidery. You may wish to place the silk print in a hoop to work the embroidery over the printed flowers.

Embroidery

Folded ribbon roses

From the 13 mm silk ribbons, make four folded ribbon roses in pink, and three folded ribbon roses in cornsilk, in assorted sizes. From the 7 mm ribbons make two folded roses in cornsilk and three folded roses in pink. Using the photo as a guide, secure each rose in place on the printed heart by bringing the #10 sharps needle up through the fabric, then stitching down through the trimmed stem of the rose, working around the stem until it is secure—approximately 5 stiches. End off after each rose.

Cream strawberry flowers

The 7 mm YLI cream silk ribbon is threaded into the #18 chenille needle to work 5 straight-stitch petals for each of the seven strawberry flowers. A French knot is worked in the centre of each flower with the 4 mm olivine silk ribbon threaded in the same needle. Complete each of these flowers by working 2-wrap French knots with Rajmahal gold silk thread and a sharps #10 needle around the ribbon knot centre. Always remember when working with any silk thread or ribbon to use only short 12 inch (30 cm) lengths.

Pink daisies

Using #10 sharps needle and a single strand of DMC 3726, stitch the daisies with lazy daisy stitch petals. Using the photo as a guide, stitch all of the daisies around the heart; some of them will only be part daisies with a few petals peeping out from behind the other flowers. A single-strand 2-wrap French knot of Rajmahal gold silk thread 45 threaded in the same needle becomes the centre of each daisy. While working with this thread, stitch the centres for the forget-me-nots in the same manner, then thread 2 strands of DMC 932 and work single-wrap French knots around each forget-me-not centre.

Rosebuds

The cornsilk and pink rosebuds are worked with 4 mm ribbons threaded in chenille needle #20 and 2 small overlapping straight stitches. Then thread 2 strands of dark green DMC 9520 into the #10 sharps needle to stem-stitch the large right-hand pink rose stems and fly-stitch the calyx around each bud.

The Judith & Kathryn silk print 'Rose Heart Wreath' used as the background for the embroidery

Ribbon leaves

Using the photo as a guide, ribbon-stitch leaves are now worked with the three different green ribbons (both 4 mm and 7 mm) threaded into the #18 chenille needle.

Fill-in flowers

Thread the #20 chenille needle with 4 mm YLI #156 cream ribbon and work small scattered flowers with a single French knot centre above the bow at the top of the heart, and randomly throughout the design. Thread a beading needle with cream sewing thread and scatter the cream embroidery beads throughout the design, stitching through each one twice to secure.

Leaves

Using the two DMC green threads alternately, soften the whole heart design by stitching single-strand lazy daisy leaves, using the photo as a guide for placement, both within the heart and outside it.

Bow

Thread the chenille #18 needle with 4 mm hand-dyed rose pink ribbon and stitch each side with a loop stitch, a straight-stitch centre and a twisted straight stitch for each tail, being careful not to stitch through any of the ribbon. Using a matching sewing thread and a sharps #12 needle, catch the ribbon into position with tiny holding stitches. Also catch any ribbon ends back underneath the embroidered area, otherwise they will show when the piece is stretched for mounting.

Framing

Take the finished work to a professional framer for mounting in a deep box frame.

Heart Disease in Australia

Cardiovascular disease is responsible for more than 40 per cent of all deaths in Australia, claiming one life every ten minutes. This means that cardiovascular disease (including heart, stroke and vascular diseases) is Australia's biggest killer. Coronary heart disease (mostly heart attacks) is the largest single cause of death, claiming 27 825 lives in 1998. Every day, around 80 Australians die from coronary heart disease. The reality is that cardiovascular disease claims the lives of more than one in three Australians.

> **SYMPTOMS OF HEART ATTACK**
> **REQUIRE PROMPT ACTION**
> **EVERY MINUTE COUNTS**

Thanks to drugs and medical procedures such as angioplasty available in hospitals, and access to early defibrillation in case of cardiac arrest, lives can be saved. Sadly, however, too many people delay taking action, resulting in greater damage to the heart muscle and, worse still — death.

The National Heart Foundation of Australia

The Heart Foundation is an Australia-wide, non-profit, non-government health organisation, committed to fighting Australia's number one killer — heart disease, stroke and related diseases.

We are Australia's leading heart health charity, saving lives through heart research and community education programs. We are funded almost entirely by donations and gifts in wills and therefore rely on the generosity of Australians to continue our lifesaving work.

The Heart Foundation is proud of the life-saving research and health promotion programs that have made an important difference to lives of thousands of Australians over the past 40 years. The results are impressive, but there is so much more to be done as heart disease, stroke and related diseases remain Australia's biggest killer.

How to have a healthy heart

'Risk factors' for heart disease are characteristics that increase our chance of developing heart disease. These include:

Cigarette smoking
High blood cholesterol
Physical inactivity
Diabetes
High blood pressure
Overweight

Being male, increasing age and having a family history of early death from heart disease are also contributory risk factors for developing heart disease.

The best way of reducing the risk of developing heart disease, or to help prevent it getting worse if it already exists, is to reduce or remove the risk factors over which we have some control. To do this, have ongoing heart disease risk assessments regularly undertaken by your general practitioner, and lead a healthy lifestyle following these five guidelines:

1. Stop smoking

Smoking reduces the amount of oxygen in your blood and damages the walls of the arteries. Stopping smoking is the single most important thing you can do to reduce your risk of coronary heart disease. For more information on quitting smoking, call the Quitline on 131 848.

2. Enjoy healthy eating

Cholesterol and fat contribute to the deposits which build up in the artery walls and cause disease. You can help lower your blood cholesterol level and limit further artery clogging by reducing the amount of saturated fats you eat. Saturated fats are found in fatty meats, full cream dairy products, butter, two common vegetable oils (coconut and palm oils), most fried take-away foods and commercially baked products. Replace saturated fats with moderate amounts of monounsaturated and polyunsaturated fats such as canola, olive, sunflower and soybean oils.

Healthy eating is also about choosing mainly plant-based foods such as bread, cereals, rice, pasta, vegetables, fruits and legumes (dried peas, beans and lentils), with moderate amounts of lean meats, poultry, fish and reduced-fat dairy products. (Note: In addition to healthy eating, long-term medication may be required to lower your blood cholesterol level.)

3. Be physically active

The body is designed to move, and regular, moderate physical activity is good for the heart. Being active is also a great way to have fun. Physical activity can also help control other risk factors such as high blood pressure and being overweight. The Heart

Foundation recommends that people include 30 minutes or more of moderate intensity physical activity (such as brisk walking) on most, if not all, days of the week, for health benefits. This amount of activity can be accumulated in several shorter bursts, such as three 10-minute walks.

4. Control blood pressure

High blood pressure can strain your heart and speed up the progression of coronary heart disease. Have regular blood pressure checks. If your blood pressure is high, reduce salt intake, limit alcohol to two drinks or less daily and follow your doctor's advice. Long-term medication may be required to manage high blood pressure.

5. Lose weight if you need to

Being overweight, and carrying too much weight around the waist, are risk factors for coronary heart disease and diabetes. Healthy eating and being physically active assist weight loss. Your doctor can advise you on your waist measurement goal. For more information on preventing heart disease, please contact Heartline on 1300 362 787.

Heart Foundation Information—Heartline

Thanks to many generous donations and bequests, the Heart Foundation has been able to provide accurate and up to date information for health professionals, people with heart disease and the general public for over 40 years. Last year alone, 1.2 million booklets, information sheets and brochures were distributed through Heartline.

Heartline is the Heart Foundation's national telephone information service. For the cost of a local call, callers can seek advice on issues such as heart disease and stroke, healthy eating, blood pressure, cholesterol, quitting smoking, physical activity and heart surgery.

The Heart Foundation's Heartline call centre is staffed by trained health professionals. This enables the Foundation to provide vital, accessible health information for heart patients, their families and the wider community, as well as the latest heart health information for health professionals.

Heart Foundation Website
www.heartfoundation.com.au

The Heart Foundation also has a comprehensive range of heart health information on its website. Divided into sections for the general public and health professionals, the website hosts the latest heart and stroke statistics, and general heart information, as well as the latest guidelines for cardiologists and GPs.

World Heart Health Organisations

The growing incidence of cardiovascular disease (heart disease and stroke) is a worldwide problem.

- **Cardiovascular disease accounts for 30 per cent of deaths worldwide.**
- **One out of every three deaths (17 million deaths per annum) is from cardiovascular disease.**
- **Much of the suffering and death from cardiovascular disease can be prevented.**
- **Strategies exist to reduce death and disability in individual patients and populations.**

Heart Foundations and Associations around the world work in similar ways to help people in different countries achieve a longer and better life through prevention and control of heart disease and stroke. They come together to share knowledge and experience to reduce the numbers of people developing the disease and increase the numbers of people surviving heart attack and stroke.

Each organisation works to achieve this through supporting medical research and scientific enquiry, educating and training clinical specialists, general practitioners and community members, and advocating for government support and activity.

To access information, advice and publications about cardiovascular disease, nutrition, smoking cessation and exercise, you can you can go to the website or email the Heart Foundation in your country listed below. Other organisations contact details may be located at the World Heart Federation website — visit www.worldheart.org

Heart Foundations around the world are supported by the generosity of individuals and companies. Making a donation to your local Heart Foundation will assist in the funding of medical research and implementation of community heart health programs.

AMERICAN HEART ASSOCIATION

President: Lawrence Sadwin MD
Tel. (+1 214) 373 6300
Fax (+1 214) 373 9818
E-mail: inquire@americanheart.org
Home page: www.americanheart.org

ARGENTINE HEART FOUNDATION

Tel. (+54 11) 4961 9388
Fax (+54 11) 4961 6520
E-mail: funcargen@canopus.com.ar
Home page: www.funcargen.org.ar

BELGIAN HEART LEAGUE

President: Paul de Souter
Tel. (+32 2) 649 8537
Fax (+32 2) 649 2828
E-mail: ligue.cardio.liga@euronet.be
Home page: www.eurohealth.org.uk/belgium

BRAZILIAN HEART FOUNDATION (FUNCOR)

President: Celso Amodeo MD
Tel./fax: (+55 11) 829 6438
E-mail: funcor@cardiol.br

THE BRITISH HEART FOUNDATION

President: Sir Richard Lloyd Bt
14 Fitzhardinge Street
London W1H 6DH
Tel. (+44 20) 7935 0185
Fax (+44 20) 7486 5820
E-mail: directorate@bhf.org.uk
Home page: http://www.bhf.org.uk

HEART AND STROKE FOUNDATION OF CANADA

President: Allan Lefever
Tel. (+1 613) 569 4361
Fax (+1 613) 569 3278
E-mail: itstaff@hsf.ca
Home page: www.heartandstroke.ca

CHILEAN HEART FOUNDATION

President: Mario Alvo
Tel. (+56 2) 633 9241
Fax (+56 2) 633 9241
E-mail: funcar@entelchile.net

CYPRUS HEART FOUNDATION

President: Hagop Keheyan
Tel. (+357 2) 762 762
Fax (+357 2) 757 744
E-mail: cyheart@spidernet.com.cy

DANISH HEART FOUNDATION

President: Joergen Fischer Hansen MD
Tel. (+45 33) 93 1788
Fax (+45 33) 93 1245
E-mail: post@hjerteforeningen.dk

FINNISH HEART ASSOCIATION

President: Jussi Huttunen MD
Tel. (+358 9) 752 7521
Fax (+358 9) 752 75250
E-mails: sydanliitto@sydanliitto.fi
Home page: www.sydanliitto.fi

FRENCH HEART FOUNDATION

President: Daniel Thomas MD
Tel. (+33 1) 4490 8383
Fax (+33 1) 4387 9812
E-mail: presse@fedecardio.com
Home page: www.fedecardio.com

GERMAN HEART FOUNDATION

President: Hans-Jürgen Becker MD
Tel. (+49 69) 955 1280
Fax (+49 69) 955 1283 / 13
E-mail: hertzstiftung@compuserve.com
Home page: www.herzstiftung.de

HELLENIC HEART FOUNDATION

President: Metropolitan of Thebes and Levadia
Ieronymos
Tel. (+30 1) 640 1477 or 645 0118
Fax (+30 1) 640 1478
E-mail: elikar@aias.gr
Home page: www.elikar.gr

THE HONG KONG HEART FOUNDATION, LTD.

Chairman: The Hon. Lee Quo-Wei
Tel. (+852) 2877 0564
Fax (+852) 2525 4403

HUNGARIAN NATIONAL HEART FOUNDATION
President: Sándor Timár MD
Tel. (+36 76) 481 781
Fax (+36 76) 481 219
E-mail: timars@szivalap-kh.hn
Home page: www.szivalap-kh.hu

ALL INDIA HEART FOUNDATION
President: S. Padmavati MD
Tel. (+91 11) 328 8465
Fax (+91 11) 622 5733
E-mail: padmavat@del2.vsnl.net.in

HEART FOUNDATION OF INDONESIA
President: Mrs Krisnina Akbar Tandjune
Tel. (+62 21) 390 9176
Fax (+62 21) 314 4670
E-mail: yayasan@inaheart.or.id
Home page: www.inaheart.com

IRISH HEART FOUNDATION
President: Brian Maurer MD
Tel. (+353 1) 668 5001
Fax (+353 1) 668 5896
E-mail: info@irishheart.ie

ISRAEL HEART SOCIETY
President: Babeth Rabinowitz MD
Tel. (+972 3) 6122 577
Fax (+972 3) 6122 588
E-mail: ihs@israel-heart.org.il
Home page: www.israel-heart.org.il

ITALIAN HEART FOUNDATION
President: Rodolfo Paoletti MD
Tel. (+39 02) 2900 5297
Fax (+39 02) 2900 7018
E-mail: info@fondazionecuore.it
Home page: www.fondazionecuore.it

JAPAN HEART FOUNDATION
President: Takuji Shidachi
Tel. (+81 3) 3201 0810
Fax (+81 3) 3213 3920
E-mail: info@jhf.or.jp
Home page: www.jhf.or.jp/

THE HEART FOUNDATION OF MALAYSIA
President: Haji Omar Ong Yoke Lin
Tel. (+60 3) 2143 4709 / 4710
Fax (+60 3) 2142 6059
E-mail: jantung@tm.net.my
Home page: www.yjm.org.my

NETHERLANDS HEART FOUNDATION
President: J. E. Jansen
Tel (+31 70) 315 5555
Fax (+31 70) 335 2826
E-mail: info@hartstichting.nl
Home page: www.hartstichting.nl

THE NATIONAL HEART FOUNDATION OF NEW ZEALAND
President: Peter McQueen
Tel. (+64 9) 571 9191
Fax (+64 9) 571 9190
E-mail: info@nhf.org.nz
Home page: www.heartfoundation.org.nz

NORWEGIAN COUNCIL ON CARDIOVASCULAR DISEASES
President: Terje Skjaerpe MD
Tel. (+47 23) 12 0000
Fax (+47 23) 12 0001
E-mail: post@nasjonalforeningen.no
Home page: www.nasjonalforeningen.no

PAKISTAN HEART FOUNDATION
President: Muhammad Ilyas MD
Tel. (+92 91) 810 551
Fax (+92 21) 810 451 / 845 234
E-mail: phf@pes.comsats.net.pk
Home page: www.phf.sdnpk.org

HEART FOUNDATION OF THE PHILIPPINES
President: Augusto A Camara MD
Tel. (+63 2) 925 2401 ext. 2236
Fax (+63 2) 928 1414
E-mail: hfphil@info.com.ph

PORTUGUESE HEART FOUNDATION
President: Manuel Oliveira Carrageta MD
Tel. (+351 21) 381 5000
Fax (+351 21) 387 3331
E-mail: fpcardio@mail.telepac.pt
Home page: www.fpcardiologia.pt

SAUDI HEART ASSOCIATION
President: Mansour Al-Nozha MD
Tel. (+966 1) 467 1434
Fax (+966 1) 467 2553
E-mail: saudhass@ksu.edu.sa

SINGAPORE NATIONAL HEART ASSOCIATION
Chairman: Low Lip-Ping MD
Tel. (+65) 324 0226
Fax (+65) 324 0225
E-mail: info@snha.org
Home page: www.snha.org

SLOVAK REPUBLIC 'HEART TO HEART' LEAGUE
President: Ján Slezák MD
Tel./Fax (+421 7) 39 4210
E-mail: slezak@up.upsav.sk

SLOVENIAN HEART FOUNDATION
President: Josip Turk MD
Tel. (+386 61) 136 95 62 / 63
Fax (+386 61) 136 87 84
E-mail: drustvo.zasrce@siol.net

HEART FOUNDATION OF SOUTHERN AFRICA
Director: Robert J. de Souza
Tel. (+27 21) 510 6262
Fax (+27 21) 510 6267
E-mail: heart@heartfoundation.co.za
Home page: www.heartfoundation.co.za

SPANISH HEART FOUNDATION
President: Jorge Arque Ferrari
Tel. (+34 91) 724 2373
Fax (+34 91) 724 2374
E-mail: fec@secardiologia.es
Home page: www.secardiologia.es

SWEDISH HEART LUNG FOUNDATION
President: Marianne Lundius
Tel. (+46 8) 566 24 200
Fax (+46 8) 566 24 229
E-mail: info@hjart-lungfonden.se
Home page: www.hjart-lungfonden.se

SWISS HEART FOUNDATION
President: Wilhelm Rutishauser MD
Tel. (+41 31) 388 8080
Fax (+41 31) 388 8088
E-mail: info@swissheart.ch

TAIWAN HEART FOUNDATION
Chairman: Chin-Yen Kao
Executive Director: Philip Yu-An Ding
Tel. (+886 2) 2875 7229
Fax (+886 2) 2875 3580
E-mail: yading@vghtpe.gov.tw

THE HEART FOUNDATION OF THAILAND
President: HRH Princess Maha Chakri Sirindhorn
Tel. (+66 2) 716 6658
Fax (+66 2) 716 5813
E-mail: heartfd@ksc.th.com

THE TURKISH HEART FOUNDATION
Chairman: Cetin Yildirimakin
Tel. (+90 212) 212 0707
Fax (+90 212) 212 6835
E-mail: koordinator@tkv.org.tr
Home page: www.tkv.org.tr

VIETNAM NATIONAL HEART ASSOCIATION
President: Tran do Trinh MD
Tel. (+84 4) 8697 011 / 8693 731 ext. 633
Fax (+84 4) 8691 607
E-mail: hoangvk@hn.vnn.vn

National Heart Foundation of Australia — Division addresses

NEW SOUTH WALES
Level 4, 407 Elizabeth Street
Surry Hills   NSW   2010
Tel.: (02) 9219 2444
PO Box 2222
Strawberry Hills B.C.   NSW   2012

AUSTRALIAN CAPITAL TERRITORY
Cnr Denison St & Geils Crt
Deakin   ACT   2600
Tel.: (02) 6282 5744
PO Box 220
Deakin West   ACT   2600

QUEENSLAND
557 Gregory Terrace
Fortitude Valley   QLD   4006
Tel.: (07) 3854 1696
PO Box 442
Fortitude Vally   QLD   4006

VICTORIA
411 King Street
West Melbourne   VIC   3003
Tel.: (03) 9329 8511

SOUTH AUSTRALIA
155-159 Hutt Street
Adelaide   SA   5000
Tel.: (08) 8224 2888
PO Box 7174 Hutt Street
Adelaide   SA   5000

WESTERN AUSTRALIA
334 Rokeby Road
Subiaco   WA   6008
Tel.: (08) 9388 3343
PO Box 1133
Subiaco   WA   6904

NORTHERN TERRITORY
Third Floor, Darwin Central Building
21 Knuckey Street
Darwin   NT   0800
Tel.: (08) 8981 1966
GPO Box 4363
Darwin   NT   0801

TASMANIA
86 Hampden Road
Battery Point   TAS   7000
Tel.: (03) 6224 2722
GPO Box 1312
Hobart   TAS   7001

www.heartfoundation.com.au

Heartline National Information Service
1 300 362 787

Donations to Heart Foundation
1 300 301 165